Leadership in Asia

in Asia

Challenges, Opportunities, and Strategies from Top Global Leaders

Edited by DAVE ULRICH

New York Chicago San Francisco Lisbon London Madrid Mexico City
Milan New Delhi San Juan Seoul Singapore Sydney Toronto

The *McGraw·Hill* Companies

Library of Congress Cataloging-in-Publication Data

Ulrich, Dave.
   Leadership in Asia : challenges, opportunities, and strategies from top global leaders / edited by Dave Ulrich. — 1st ed.
      p.   cm.
   Includes index.
   ISBN 978-0-07-174384-6 (alk. paper)
   1. Leadership—Asia.   2. Political leadership—Asia.   3. Asia—Economic integration.   I. Ulrich, David, 1953-

   HD57.7.L4332   2010
   796.357'64'0—dc22   2010006076

1 2 3 4 5 6 7 8 9 10 11 12 13 14   WFR/WFR   1 9 8 7 6 5 4 3 2 1 0

ISBN 978-0-07-174384-6
MHID   0-07-174384-7

Contents

Foreword

The economic transformation of Asia, propelled by the growth of China and India, presents abundant new and exciting opportunities for businesses around the world. Many global companies are establishing or expanding their presence in Asia, whether it be for the purpose of locating their senior management teams, conducting global business activities, or simply being sited within the Asian market. Increasingly, Asian enterprises that have grown rapidly in their domestic markets are seeking a global outreach.

A common challenge for these companies is human capital. To seize opportunities, grow new markets and operate across borders and cultures, companies need a strong talent bench, particularly managerial talent. The rapid growth in Asia in recent years has created a strong demand for such talent. The supply pipeline has not been able to keep up. Asian enterprises going global need their managerial talent to develop global business skills. On the other hand, MNCs growing their Asian businesses need talent that can operate effectively across markets in this region.

These demands pose a unique set of leadership and human capital challenges for business leaders and companies operating in this region. Asia's own solutions to these challenges are therefore needed. Companies seeking to sustain rapid growth in this region must develop their talent base in a strategic and proactive manner. Similarly, Asian companies going global need to nurture corporate leaders who are ready to take on global challenges.

With a cosmopolitan workforce and being a home for many MNCs and Asian enterprises, Singapore can play a role as companies seek Asian solutions for addressing the strategic human capital challenges in the region. The Singapore Ministry of Manpower and Workforce Development Agency organized the annual Singapore Human Capital Summit to achieve a confluence of leading ideas, knowledge and practices on human capital development for Asia. The Summit brings together global and regional business and HR leaders, as well as thought leaders, for a high-level discussion on the strategies for dealing with human capital challenges in Asia.

Another initiative organized by Singapore is the Executive Roundtable. This is a strategic conversation involving top corporate leaders on human capital and leadership development in Asia. The inaugural Roundtable, themed "Leadership Challenges, Opportunities and Strategies for New Asia," was held on 4 May 2009. Thirteen global business leaders, thought leaders and senior HR practitioners spent a day deliberating on and identifying key people challenges in Asia. They also articulated key strategies to address these challenges and enhance corporate competitiveness.

This book condenses the main ideas from the discussion at the inaugural Executive Roundtable, as well as best practices from the participating companies. It aims to further this important strategic conversation on leadership development and human capital management in Asia. I would like to extend my sincere appreciation to the 13 business and thought leaders for contributing to the important topic of thought leadership in Asia and for their valuable contributions to this book. I would also like to express my gratitude to Professor Dave Ulrich, Professor of Business from Ross School of Business, Univer-sity of Michigan, who did an outstanding job in facilitating the Roundtable. He is also the editor who has so capably woven this book together. In addition, I want to thank Mr. Chan Heng Kee, Chief Executive for the Singapore Workforce Development Agency, for hosting the Executive Roundtable and for his helpful comments on this book. I also want to extend my appreciation to my able colleagues, Low Peck Kem, Shirlyn Ng and Albert Foo, whose tireless efforts made this book possible.

I hope that this collection of ideas and perspectives will inspire corporate leaders in Asia and beyond to further develop their own leadership and human capital strategies in their organizations. It is important for us to continually generate new knowledge and advance the thinking on human capital strategies, as well as to contextualize the knowledge for application by Asian-based companies. This will be an area that Singapore seeks to continue to contribute to.

Leo Yip
Permanent Secretary
Ministry of Manpower, Singapore

List of Contributors

**Dave Ulrich** is a Professor of Business at the Ross School of Business at the University of Michigan and a partner at The RBL Group (www.rbl.net), a consulting firm that helps organizations and leaders deliver value. Ulrich studies how organizations build capabilities of speed, learning, collaboration, accountability, talent and leadership through leveraging human resources. He has helped generate award-winning databases that assess alignment between strategies, human resource practices and HR competencies.

Ulrich has published more than 200 articles and book chapters and co-authored over 20 books on topics in leadership and human resources, including *HR Transformation* (2009); *The Leadership Code* (2008); *HR Competencies* (2008); and *Leadership Brand* (2007). He has been ranked the most influential person in HR by *HR Magazine* and the #1 Management Educator & Guru by *BusinessWeek*, and listed in *Forbes* as one of the "world's top five" business coaches.

Fergus Balfour is the Chief Operating Officer at Unilever Foodsolutions Asia, Africa and Middle East. During the 35 years that he has been with Unilever, Balfour has worked in many of the companies' different businesses, ranging from the conventional, such as detergents, ice cream and other food products, to service and cosmetic businesses as well as joint ventures, including that with Panasonic Corporation (formerly Matsushita). Most of his professional experience has been in marketing and general management; Balfour has also led the leadership development initiative for the global company. The latter was a five-year stint that allowed him to observe the many different styles of leadership in Unilever, and to be convinced that high-quality leadership is the key to producing extraordinary results. As such, he demands strong views, independence and quick action of the people he works with, and is impatient with bureaucracy and a lack of commitment or decision making.

J. Stewart Black is the Associate Dean for Executive Development Programs for the Americas region and a professor in the area of leadership at INSEAD. He is also the Director of the INSEAD Center for Human Resources in Asia. Black's research focuses on human capital, global leaders and managing change. In addition, he consults with a wide variety of companies across the globe but also does considerable work in Asia, where he has spent over a decade, especially in Japan, Hong Kong and Singapore. He is the author of 11 books and more than 50 articles and chapters.

Gerald Chan is the Country Head and CEO of UBS Singapore and Senior Client Relationship Director for UBS's Fixed Income, Currencies and Commodities (FICC) business. He has been with UBS for 15 years. As the business is expanding, Chan is focusing on deepening relationships with the bank's key institutional clients, banks and corporates in Asia Pacific.

Between 1994 and 1997, Chan headed the FX Sales for South and Southeast Asia, then moved to London in 1998 to work on the global proprietary-trading desk. He relocated to Hong Kong in 2000 to become the Head of FX Sales for North Asia. In 2001, he was appointed Regional Head of Business Development for Asia Pacific, based in Singapore. In 2002, Chan was appointed Head of FX Distribution for Asia Pacific. Chan has worked closely with industry and regulatory bodies and advised the Government of Singapore on the country's development as a financial center.

Liak Teng Lit is the Chief Executive Officer of Alexandra Hospital and CEO-designate for Khoo Teck Puat Hospital. He has been in the healthcare industry since 1977 when he graduated with a BS (Pharmacy) from the Department of Pharmacy, National University of Singapore, and began his career as a pharmacist. He has held senior positions at various hospitals, including as CEO at the Changi General Hospital and Toa Payoh Hospital. Liak serves on the boards of NTUC Childcare, Pathlight School and NorthLight School, and on the Advisory Panel of the School of Information

Systems at the Singapore Management University and the Singapore Human Resources Institute. He also sits on several committees, including Water Networks, Incentives & Grants/Lifelong Learning Fund Advisory Council, Institute of Service Excellence @ SMU (ISES) Governing Council, Nanyang Polytechnic Health Sciences Advisory Committee, Community Chest and the Silver Industry Committee.

Liak also holds an MBA from the National University of Singapore, as well as an MS (Pharmaceutical Sciences) from the University of Aston, Birmingham, UK.

 **Liew Mun Leong** is the President and CEO of CapitaLand Group and a Board member of CapitaLand Limited. He is Deputy Chairman of CapitaMall Trust Management Limited, CapitaCommercial Trust Management Limited, CapitaRetail China Trust Management Limited and Ascott Residence Trust Management Limited. He is also Chairman of CapitaLand China Executive Committee, which coordinates and aligns CapitaLand's investments, operations, branding and resources in China, and a Director of CapitaLand Hope Foundation, the Group's philanthropic arm. Liew is at present Chairman of Changi Airport Group (Singapore) Private Limited and a Director of Singapore Exchange Limited. In 2006, Liew was named Outstanding CEO of the Year (Singapore Business Awards). In 2007, he was conferred the CEO of the Year Award in *The Business Times*' Singapore Corporate Awards. In 2008, Liew was named Asia's Best Executive of 2008 (Singapore) by *Asiamoney* and Best CEO in Asia (Property) by *Institutional Investor*.

Girija Pande is the Executive VP and the Head of the Asia Pacific operations of Tata Consultancy Services (TCS), one of Asia's largest IT companies, with nearly U.S. $6 billion in revenue and over 143,000 software consultants based in 42 countries. Currently based in Singapore, Pande is Chairman of TCS Asia Pacific Pte. Ltd., a Singapore-registered holding company and the TCS headquarters for Asia Pacific. He oversees TCS businesses in 13 Asia Pacific countries, including Greater China, Japan, ASEAN and Australia/New Zealand. Pande is a member of International Enterprise (IE) Singapore's Network India Steering Committee, chairman of the India Business Forum (IBF), and member of the Singapore Infocomm Development Authority's (IDA) Infocomm Manpower Council. He is also on the advisory boards of Nanyang Business School at Nanyang Technological University, Singapore, and of a private equity fund investing in India.

Saw Phaik Hwa is the President and CEO of SMRT Corporation Limited, the first multi-modal public transport operator in Singapore offering mass rapid transit, light rail, bus and taxi services. With her extensive experience in international corporate business, Saw offers a fresh approach to the way transport services are managed and operated in Singapore. She is instrumental in the development and implementation of key initiatives in the SMRT group of companies, which include system revamps to transform commercial assets and the establishment of an office in Dubai to develop opportunities in the Middle East. Saw also champions corporate initiatives for sustainable development, including SMRT Corporate Volunteer Program, SMRT Silver Tribute Fund, and SMRT is Green.

Saw has a Bachelor of Science (Honors) in Biochemistry from the National University of Singapore and has undergone an advanced management program at the University of Hawaii.

 **Peter Smith** is the global leader of Mercer's talent and succession practice, and a principal consultant in Mercer's Human Capital business. Based in Australia, Smith's client base extends through Asia, the Middle East, the Americas and Europe, and includes major financial, construction, retail, telecommunications providers and government agencies. He has held HR management roles with Shell International and Mars Inc., was the founder and Managing Director of HR Partnering Proprietary Limited and joined Mercer in September 2006. Peter has broad HR management experience derived over 25 years in senior corporate and business consulting roles, including ten years' specialist consulting to major Australian and international clients in talent and succession management and in associated management information systems. Peter helps clients shape their talent and succession practices and facilitates their board and executive team talent workshops.

 **Jessica Tan Soon Neo** is the Managing Director of Microsoft Singapore. She is responsible for developing and driving growth strategies for the company's business in Singapore, as well as deepening relationships with partners, customers and employees. She also focuses on leading Microsoft's ongoing corporate citizenship efforts in the country, which includes Microsoft's efforts to becoming a trusted industry partner that works with businesses, communities and governments to help advance social and economic well-being.

In May 2006, Tan was elected Member of Parliament in Singapore for the East Coast Group Representation Constituency (GRC). In addition, she is the Chairman of the East Coast Town Council and of the Finance and Trade & Industry Government Parliamentary Committee (GPC), and is a member of the Manpower GPC. Jessica graduated from the National University of Singapore in 1989 with a Bachelor of Social Sciences (Honors).

Wee Chow Hou is the Professor and Head of the Division of Marketing and International Business and Chairman of the Nanyang Executive Programs, at the Nanyang Business School, Nanyang Technological University in Singapore. He is also the Honorary Professor, Faculty of Management, at Xiamen University in China. Prior to joining NTU, Wee was Professor of Business Policy, Dean of the Faculty of Business Administration, and Director of the Graduate School of Business (1990–1999) at the National University of Singapore.

Wee has consulted for and conducted executive programs for more than 250 major organizations in Asia, North America and Europe, including *Fortune* 500 companies and major corporations such as Hewlett-Packard, Singapore Airlines, and Motorola Corporation. He is currently a Board Director of several publicly listed companies in Singapore. He has also published more than 300 papers in various international, regional and local journals and proceedings.

Patrick M. Wright is the William J. Conaty Professor of Strategic Human Resources and Director. Prior to joining Cornell University, New York in 1999, he held positions as Associate Professor and Coordinator of the MS in HR Management program at the College of

Business at Texas A&M University, and Assistant Professor of Management in the College of Business at University of Notre Dame. He holds a BA in Psychology from Wheaton College, and an MBA and a PhD in Organizational Behavior/Human Resource Management from Michigan State University. From 2000 to 2007, Wright served on the Board of Directors for the Society for Human Resource Management (SHRM) Foundation. For his leadership in the field, he was inducted as a Fellow of the U.S. National Academy of Human Resources in 2005. Wright teaches, conducts research and consults in the area of strategic human resource management (HRM), focusing on how firms use people as a source of competitive advantage.

Arthur Yeung is an Associate Dean at the China Europe International Business School (CEIBS), where he has launched a CEO Learning Consortium where CEOs from more than 30 leading firms in China share best practices on issues critical to business growth and success in China. He is also a Director at the Center of Organizational and People Excellence (COPE), which researches and benchmarks best practices related to talent management and organizational effectiveness.

Before his recent return to academia, Yeung was the Chief HR Officer of the Acer Group. As one of the five-member Transition Management Team, he actively contributed to the launch of several major change initiatives, including downsizing, turning the manufacturing arm into a separate publicly listed company, and transforming New Acer into a performance-driven, customer-centric company.

For his contributions, Yeung was elected "HR Executive of the Year" by *SmartFortune Magazine* (China) and recognized as one of the next-generation "Executive Development Gurus" by the *Business Horizon* magazine (U.S.).

CHAPTER 1

Introduction
Leadership in Asia

Dave Ulrich

The Asian region has grown exponentially in the last decade. It has been described as a juggernaut because what happens in Asia affects the world. As Asian countries, industries and organizations undergo economic, social, technological and demographic changes, the quality of leadership will be a key to responding to those challenges. In numerous surveys of CEOs and political leaders about the primary challenges in securing their future, the importance of building future leaders is cited.[1] Countries and companies with high-quality leaders will make choices to enable them to anticipate and respond more rapidly to change.

There are many ways to figure out what it means to have high-quality leaders who respond to unique Asian challenges. Some collect large data sets to offer empirical evidence about what Asian leaders need to learn and accomplish. Others have relied more on in-depth case studies to spotlight excellent Asian leaders and to generalize principles from these exemplars. Others have crafted thoughtful theories

■ *1* ■

that define quality of leadership in the Asian context. Each of these approaches begins with an understanding of what is unique about Asia. While general leadership principles may apply across time, geographies and industries, it is important to adapt these principles to the unique context of Asian commercial, private and government organizations.

To articulate future leadership requirements for Asian organizations, the Singapore Ministry of Manpower (MOM) sponsored an Executive Roundtable. Attendees were a mix of industry CEOs throughout Asia with extensive expertise, academics who had done theory building and research on leadership in the Asian context and consultants who had translated ideas into practice throughout Asia. The question that these thought leaders addressed was: "How do we build leadership and human capital in Asia to help companies succeed?" The intent of this Roundtable was to generate ideas that would capture emerging trends and themes in Asian leadership.

Participants in this Roundtable were essentially an Asian leadership focus group. Each participant brought unique expertise to the challenge of building leadership in Asia that helps companies to succeed. Each of the CEOs presented some of his or her business challenges, then talked about what these challenges suggested for leadership to be able to respond. Each of the thought leaders (academics and consultants) shared their theory, research and experience in helping Asian firms build leadership and human capital for business success. Collectively, the shared insight of industry and government executives (with deep knowledge about their company and industry) and of academics and consultants (with theory and research across firms) offer a unified perspective on what effective leadership means in the Asian context.

This volume is a compilation of the ideas shared by these thought leaders. Each individual contributor has been asked to capture from his or her experience – either inside a company as a business leader or across companies as a consultant or academic – the key insight that determines effective Asian leadership for the future.

To frame the scope of effective leadership in Asia, we need to clarify a few terms. Leadership is not just the individual or executive team at the top of the organization. Leadership is a capability shared throughout the organization and individuals who work as business, country or function managers may operate as leaders. Anyone who is charged with getting work done by guiding the behaviors of others would be considered a leader. This definition obviously includes senior executives whose decisions may affect hundreds or thousands of employees throughout an organization. It also would include a leader of a new product who is charged to bring together individuals to design and deliver a product or service. It might include the head of finance, IT or HR staff area responsible for accomplishing work through combining the skills of others. It might include a country manager who shapes a strategy for doing business in an emerging or a mature market. Leadership is by definition a team sport, which requires coordinating the action of individuals towards a common goal.

It is also important to realize that "Asia" is an amalgamation of countries, companies, cultures and contexts. India, Japan, Malaysia, China, South Korea, Singapore and the Philippines are enormously different. These countries differ by cultural heritage, political systems, population demographics, social structures and levels of economic maturity. It is difficult, if not impossible, to create a uniform "Asian" view of leadership that applies equally in each country.

Nevertheless, there are some common principles that apply to the Asian context more than North America, Europe, the Middle East or Latin America. Understanding the unique setting of Asia business offers a perspective on the leadership insight shared in this volume. One of the temptations is to compare and contrast "Asian" leadership with "European, North American or another region's" leadership and suggest that one is better (or worse) than the other. What we believe is that global learning on leadership will help leaders to respond to paradoxes. For example, it is not just that organizations might move from entrepreneurial (more innovative and creative) to managerial (disciplined and process driven) leadership, but to learn how to do both. As we review eight unique characteristics of the Asian context, we want to highlight the paradoxes that this setting may pose for future Asian leaders. These eight **Asian Leadership Paradoxes** are the issues that the thought leaders address in their chapters for this book. These are the ideas around which Asian leaders of the future will develop capacity and insight. These paradoxes will become the criteria for how Asian leaders anticipate and respond to changing business conditions (see Table 1.1).

1. Organization type: Asian organizations represent multiple organization types

Traditionally, large Asian organizations were either State-Owned Enterprises (SOEs) or Privately Owned Enterprises (POEs). SOEs not only operated in the public sector, but also had influence in energy, media, communications, financial service and other domains of the more traditional private sector. Many of the stereotypical images of the tradi-

TABLE 1-1. ASIAN ORGANIZATION/LEADERSHIP TRENDS

Dimension of Asian Context	Traditional View	Emerging View	Leadership Paradox: What leaders need to manage for emerging human capital trends
Organization type	State-Owned Enterprise (SOE) or family business	Privately Owned Enterprise (POE) or MNC	Recognize and manage at the same time different organization types that exist within the Asian business community
Family centricity	Family-based organizations	Professionally managed	Learn to respect and work within family-centric enterprises while creating professionally managed organizations
Success and reinvention	Rapid recent growth	Reinvent for future growth	Relish recent successes and renew to prepare for the future
Governance	Political masters/ Bureaucracy	Simple and accountable	Recognize bureaucratic, hierarchical and political complexity and create flexible, agile and simple organizations

TABLE 1-1. *(continued)*

Dimension of Asian Context	Traditional View	Emerging View	Leadership Paradox: What leaders need to manage for emerging human capital trends
Hierarchy	Monopoly with strong centralized control	Market-based organization with high agility	Gain the internal efficiencies of working in a protected market and the external responsiveness of a market-based organization
Time horizon	Long term	Short term	Think long term to envision a future and act today to survive the present
Polite and respectful culture	Grace/ Courtesy	Results/ Courage	Maintain grace, courtesy and an Asian style, but be rigorous and demanding, and take risks
Talent	Attract talent with systematic process	Adapt to individual talent requirement	Invest in future talent and respond to today's talent needs

tional Asian organization would be pegged to these SOEs: large, bureaucratic, hierarchical and slow moving. In addition to these large SOEs, many Asian organizations were small family businesses (POEs) serving a local community clientele.

In recent years, organization types have evolved in the Asian business landscape. Privately Owned Enterprises (POEs) have shifted from small family businesses with individual entrepreneurs and expanded to become larger national, regional and at times global POEs. These POEs often start out (and continue) as family-based businesses, with a strong-willed, dynamic and risk-taking entrepreneur who establishes and grows a business. These businesses move quickly into new markets and pass from generation to generation through family connections. Traditionally, they have been small shops, restaurants, or other consumer or service enterprises. Today, POEs have grown up in almost every industry and many are large, global and multigenerational. Different countries experience different versions of POEs. In Singapore, most of the privately owned enterprises are family owned. However, in China, quite a number of privately owned enterprises are nonfamily owned but founded by a group of cofounders (due to limited funding and expertise of entrepreneurs in that period of China). Hence, a family-owned business is a subset of privately owned enterprises. Nevertheless, the tensions and transition from entrepreneurial firms (privately owned enterprises, including family-owned businesses) to professionally run companies are real and challenging.

Multinational corporations (MNCs) have increasingly moved into Asia with the increased economic growth and business opportunities available. Almost every large global firm in every industry is represented in Asia, from automotive to technology to lodging to healthcare to retail to media. These MNCs are often divisions reporting to the headquarters in a home country. Leaders often transfer in and out and work to bring products, practices and processes from the rest of the world into the Asian market. Each of these three organization types (SOE, POE, MNC) is different in its funding, governance, culture, succession and ultimately leadership. What may fit in one organization type may not fit in another. For example, a primary leadership requirement might differ:

- SOEs: garner political support to a direction and protect one's position
- POEs: manage innovation, growth and family succession
- MNCs: gain resources from headquarters, transfer knowledge into and out of Asian context

Obviously, management of each organization type requires different leadership skills.

Asian Leadership Paradox 1: Recognize and manage at the same time different organization types that exist within the Asian business community

2. Family centricity: Asian work often occurs within family groups

As suggested above, many Asian firms are family-centered. This includes the many small businesses where families found and operate restaurants, retail and other small enterprises. But it also includes the entrepreneurial and growing enterprises where second-, third- and fourth-generation leaders remain within the family.

Family values are central across the Asian context. Loyalty to family remains an important and enduring value. It is not uncommon for three generations to live together and stay close through personal and professional ties. When families also have ownership of companies, these companies have the luxury of being very entrepreneurial. They often fund growth through debt more than equity which means they only have to convince a limited set of debt holders about the viability of their strategy whereas publicly traded companies financed through equity have to convince unknown investors of their long-term viability. This enables family-centric firms to take more risks and have a longer-term view.

Family companies have a succession challenge of passing the business from one generation to another. This includes managing and valuing diversity which creates new approaches to business even when most leaders of the company come from the same family background. In addition, succession within families requires working to help make sure that future leaders have the competencies for leading large complex global organizations. By definition, family enterprises have a limited pool of senior talent (often family members) and must work extra hard to have professional managers who know the latest management practices.

Asian Leadership Paradox 2: Learn to respect and work within family-centric enterprises while creating professionally managed organizations

3. Success and reinvention: Asian economies and companies have relished recent successes

In the last decade, economic growth has helped businesses flourish throughout Asia. While prosperity and growth are clearly better than the alternatives of scarcity and decline, prosperity has inherent challenges. Prosperity expands boundaries but comes with challenges.

Prosperity may require new leadership skills. Asian companies that have grown up in Asia now become regional and even global. This means that successful countries or regional companies now need to have leadership and organization skills to compete outside their home markets. The types of leadership for a local company may not suffice for a global company.

Prosperity may hide underlying weak leadership abilities. A company may be growing so quickly that no matter what the leader does, it is successful. This may keep the leader from learning how to make difficult decisions. Most companies that have sustained success do so in both up and down markets. Most leaders are truly successful after they have struggled through the throes and woes of failure. We grow more from difficult situations than from those that we are able to handle easily.

Prosperity may lead to arrogance. Over time, when a company or a country has had prosperity for many years, the leaders in those organizations may begin to think that they know how to succeed and they quit learning. When leaders start thinking they have the answers more than they ask questions, when they are more focused on themselves than the customers they serve, when they focus on their recent successes more than on future challenges, and when they isolate themselves from the customers of their services, they have allowed prosperity to lead to arrogance. These leaders are likely to struggle and not adapt to changing conditions.

Prosperity may lead to lethargy. The political philosopher Toynbee said that there is a "liability of success" in that successful people may not be as ambitious as they should have been or take as many risks. In the family-owned enterprise business, it is often said the first-generation leader defines the business, the second-generation creates it, the third expands it, and the fourth often loses it. The liability of the fourth generation is that sometimes prosperity leads to someone being not as aggressive as he or she might have been.

As Asian leaders have experienced success and enormous recent prosperity, they need to continue to renew and reinvent themselves to avoid these limitations of prosperity. What succeeded in the previous two decades may not work in the following decade.

Asian Leadership Paradox 3: Relish recent successes and renew to prepare for the future

4. Governance: Asian organizations must learn to work within the political bureaucracy

The boundary between public and private sectors is often permeable in most Asian countries. There often exists an "old boy" network where leaders know each other through school and military experiences and connections. Leaders may move between public and private sector roles.

The public sector often relies on more hierarchical, bureaucratic and political processes to govern work. Success is defined through rules and regulations that create political, social and economic stability. Permanent secretaries and ministers succeed by mitigating risks and by gaining political support for their decisions. These political masters have great influence on the future of their country by allocating resources to targeted industries and companies and shaping public opinion. Their agenda is to create political, social and economic stability, so the decision-making processes often move slowly with safeguards built in to ensure prudent risk. With stability and continuity as their goals, they often seek consistency and constancy in how they do their work. Public confidence and opinion are the ultimate measures of their success.

Private sector success often depends on speed and agility as decisions must be made quickly to respond to competitive threats. Success comes from targeting and creating new market opportunities quicker than competitors. Leaders in these organizations rise to the top by their ability to assess and take innovative risks that differentiate their firm from their competitors. With innovation and uniqueness as their goals, these leaders often encourage diversity, debate and differentiation. Gaining marketplace success through customer share and investor money defines success.

Bridging the political past with the marketplace future requires Asian leaders to live in a world of organization paradox. They need to understand and work within the hierarchical and bureaucratic political domains that drive stability while learning.

Asian Leadership Paradox 4: Recognize bureaucratic, hierarchical and political complexity and create flexible, agile and simple organizations

5. Hierarchy: Asian organizations accept the realities of protected markets

Political systems affect how work is governed. Monopoly organizations direct where leadership attention is focused. In a pure monopoly, leaders focus inside in an attempt to ensure efficiency and control. A leader of a monopoly once shared with us this point of view, "our customers should feel privileged that we are willing to give them our precious products." Leaders work to build a clear span of control with a focus on decision rights about who makes what decisions. Monopolies gain economies of scale that lead to stability and efficiency. This internal focus works as long as the monopoly operates in a closed market where competition does not exist. Historically, some Asian countries and companies have operated out of a monopoly mindset. Within the hierarchy individuals have a clear role and place. While people are treated with great respect, there is also deference to position within the hierarchy. Titles and roles matter because they communicate place in a society structure. Status comes to those who have access to those in positions of influence. While pure monopolies seldom exist, companies still exist in protected markets where they are supported by legislation that limits full competition.

In a globally transparent world, markets exist that break up monopoly mindsets. Rather than rely on internal processes to govern work, market-based organizations must respond to customer expectations. Rules are replaced with responsiveness. Leaders focus on anticipating technology and consumer trends that will lead to products or services that customers value. Success comes when leaders focus outside to anticipate and serve customers more than inside.

As Asian organizations become an increasing part of the global community, competition will require leaders to be externally focused. Best practices are based less on the organization's heritage and more on its ability to meet customer expectations.

Asian Leadership Paradox 5: Gain the internal efficiencies of operating in a protected market and the external responsiveness of a market-based organization

6. Time horizon: Asian organizations have a longer-term view

Some of the leading Asian companies have "strategic plans" that focus on decades, not years, and focus less on specific products or services, but more on philosophies that will guide decision making over time. The long-term view of a company's position in its market requires political and social stability where the culture of immediacy may be replaced with a culture of consistency. Long-term views of an organization's position in society come from funding investments for the long term more than the short term. Longer-term views within a company encourage more stable employment than job-hopping. These long-term views that are often prevalent in Asian cultures mitigate somewhat the ups and downs of current expansion or recession.

However, as technology makes innovation more transparent and rapid, as employees are increasingly aware of their choices both inside and outside a company, and as consumers become more informed about their choices, exclusively long-term thinking has dangers. Organizations must respond quickly. A CEO told us that a company that took 50 years to build could be gone in two years if it does not react to the changing market conditions. Rapid response is often a strategic choice. For some of the Generation Y employees around the world, "long-term" may be the next job or the next move.

Asian leaders need to learn to manage this inherent paradox of long-term thinking and short-term action. Doing either exclusively will lead to trouble. Thinking only about the long-term macro global trends and missing present market opportunities will erode customer confidence and market share. Acting only on short-term fads and whims will not build sustainability. Asian leaders need to find a balance between the short and long term. If their company tends to the long term, the leaders need to gently focus more on today's decisions. If the company gets trapped into rapid response, the leaders need to shift their attention to longer-term discussions.

Asian Leadership Paradox 6: Think long term to envision a future and act today to survive the present

7. Polite and respectful culture: A culture of courtesy, grace and gentility affects how Asian organizations work

Anyone who has worked in an Asian culture recognizes the respect, grace, courtesy and gentility among the Asian people. This sense of duty and honor to treat guests and family with dignity and respect is rooted in cultural values. Working together in a cohesive team is more important than individual autonomy. When individuals act autonomously, they quietly exclude themselves from the support of their team. The feeling of ritualistic niceness pervades decision making, with subtle signals being sent when employees are out of line so as to lightly and delicately return them to the clan. This culture of courtesy shows up in airline reputations (Singapore Airlines consistently has the top reputation for in-flight service among airlines), in administrative efficiency (trains, trams and systems seem to run on time), and in political processes (former political leaders stay on as mentors to the current regimes). Asian leaders are more communal in their approach where they seek consensus and not individual glory. No success can be claimed at anyone's expense. Building sustainable networks matters more than stepping on someone to get ahead.

However, courtesy and grace cannot mask intensity and drive. As the context of business changes and Asian markets are more open to global competition and Asian firms become global players, difficult, timely and courageous decisions need to be made. Sometimes working longer hours may become a substitute for intensity, but as the world shrinks, Asian organizations must be responsive to the shifting tides of global competition.

Managing the paradox of keeping cultural courtesies and traditions while acting on competitive realities is a paradox for Asian leaders. Going too far on either dimension creates problems. Too much courtesy may lead others to take advantage of the kindness. Too much aggression may alienate leaders from their cultural heritage. Asian leaders who express courageous courtesy, graceful rigour or tough love will find that they fold cultural heritage into modern realities.

Asian Leadership Paradox 7: Maintain grace, courtesy and an Asian style, but be rigorous and demanding, and take risks

8. Talent: Asian organizations must invest in talent

Some have suggested that by age four or five, the die is cast for some Asian children. Talented children get into the top preschools, then the top elementary schools, high schools, colleges, graduate schools, and ultimately top careers. Inserting oneself into an influential career without the proper pedigree is very difficult. Asian firms invest in talent for the long term, with stable employment, shared sacrifice in recessionary times, and heavy commitment to collaborative teamwork to deliver work. It has been reported that in the U.S. automotive industry, the average functions one works in before being an officer is 1.3. In the Asian automotive industry it is 4.3. This means that Asian leaders feel connected more to the company than to their functional speciality.

Often this lifetime concern for employees comes across as benevolent patriarchy where the leader plays a parental role. In this traditional case, the leader (parent) may know what is best for you and therefore expects you to basically obey and be taken care of over the long term since you are part of the leader's "family" for the long haul. The benefits of patriarchy are longevity where job security is more important than productivity and layoffs are unlikely to occur.

However, today there is a need for leaders to treat employees in a more professional than patriarchal way. Companies are more likely to invest in employees in the short and long term. Employees share in the responsibility to manage their own careers with leaders looking out for them, but with employees also having an agency for themselves. Rather than the company dictating what work employees do, where and when employees work, and how employees work, employees may take more ownership of their own careers. This may shift the more rigid career ladders into more flexible career paths. These career paths may mean moving into and out of organizations, joining organizations mid-career or having a stronger voice of work assignments.

In addition, as the business conditions evolve, it is not enough to have an Asian talent pool for Asian companies. Asian leaders need to be able to lead their companies in Europe, Africa, and North and South America. They must be able to adapt to a global workforce with values and orientations quite different from an all-Asian employee population.

Part of future talent management may not just be selecting talented employees into the company but also offering them a meaningful employee value proposition once they are in the company. This value proposition is not only what they get but also what they give and this helps employees feel engaged through their contributions.

Part of future talent management may be recognizing that many of the next-generation employees may be more interested in personal development than corporate fidelity. Desires for work/life balance, rapid professional growth and personal learning may lead some employees to seek new career choices.

Leaders managing the past loyal employee and the emerging adaptive employee need to find ways to engage both. It is not enough to have a systematic and orderly talent management process but also to create personalized employee deals that are tailored to employee strengths. Talent flow is not just about who enters the organization but how to make sure they are contributing, learning and growing while in the organization.

Asian Leadership Paradox 8: Invest in future talent and respond to today's talent needs

What are the implications of these trends for leadership in Asia?

Clearly, these eight paradoxes are indicative, not conclusive, of human capital challenges in the Asian business context. But they offer a glimpse into the requirements for Asian leaders, both for those who are leaders within government, industry or family organizations and for those charged with building leadership across the region through theory, research and consulting. We can highlight some implications of these paradoxes.

Leadership demand. There is greater demand for leaders who understand and manage these paradoxes than there is supply. At times, in emerging markets, individuals may be moved too quickly through assignments and positions and not learn the essential lessons that are acquired at different career stages. This lack of grounding shows up when individuals move into senior positions where executive judgment should have been experienced and developed, but may not exist. Simply finding enough leaders to meet the future challenges will become an increasingly significant predictor of company success. Black (this volume) highlights that the demand for leaders in Asia will far outnumber the supply.

Leadership-shared responsibility. At some level, every individual is responsible for his or her own personal and leadership development. Without the personal ambition to lead and willingness to pay the price of being a leader, individuals will not meet the expectations of a leadership position. While individuals are accountable for their personal growth, others share in developing leaders. Leaders build leadership. The ultimate success of any individual leader is his or her ability to transfer leadership expertise to the next generation. Future leaders will face different challenges than present leaders. For today's leaders to build for tomorrow, they must prepare leaders who learn and adapt. HR professionals contribute to leadership development. While line managers are owners of the leadership pool, HR professionals are architects who build frameworks, blueprints and processes for leadership growth. External advisers also may play a role in shaping future leaders. Those who work across companies may be able to generalize experiences so that good ideas may be adapted from one setting to another. As these four stakeholders to leadership development (individuals, leaders, HR and advisors) work together, they are able to create systematic approaches to building human capital.

Leadership grooming. How do we groom and develop future talent? Investing in the next generation of leadership and talent may not be left to chance. Some have argued that we will live in a free agent talent market, where individuals will exercise choice and control over their careers, moving into and out of temporary work assignments. While this may affect a portion of the workforce, it will not be sufficient to develop future workforce and leadership needs. These individual contributors may have strong expertise, but they need to be constantly encouraged to learn to stay current, they need to be able to align their expertise with the needs of the company, and their individual skills need to be connected through teams to be fully effective. Leaders coordinate individual expertise and efforts into collective results. Companies who groom future leaders will have an advantage over companies who rely on past success.

Sharing practices and systems. In recent years, there has been a lot of work done on sharing "best practices," which means learning what one organization does and trying to move that experience to another. There are two dangers of best practices. One is that they look backwards and not forward. What was good in the past may not be good in the future. Second, and even more difficult, is that any one management practice always occurs within a system. Isolating and copying one practice that was embedded within a system and moving it to another system may not lead to the same positive result. Leaders need to learn from others not only about best practices that worked but also about best systems that offer integrated solutions to human capital problems.

Leadership change. It is almost impossible to predict the future from the present. Linear predictions are interrupted with unanticipated economic, political, social, demographic and technological disruptions. As leaders develop the capacity for continual change and responsiveness, they are less worried about what the unknown change might be and more worried about their capacity to respond to whatever change might occur.

This compilation from industry, academia and consulting diagnoses not only what is happening to leadership in the Asian context but also offers innovative and practical solutions to how leaders might respond.

Endnote

1. "The Organizational Challenges of Global Trends: A McKinsey Global Survey," *McKinsey Quarterly*, December 2007.

CHAPTER 2

What Is an Effective Leader?
The Leadership Code and Leadership Brand

Dave Ulrich[1]

Most CEO studies suggest a need for improved next-generation leadership. Most of us have personal experience that leaders matter. When we work in an organization with a talented leader, we are not only more productive, it feels different. When we buy products from a company with talented leaders, we sense responsiveness and often buy more. When we invest in companies with strong leaders, we have confidence in their future success. Simply stated, leadership matters. We know it empirically and viscerally.

Throughout Asia, where emerging markets are growing rapidly, where State-Owned Enterprises and Privately Owned (Family) Enterprises must respond to global requirements, and where change is rampant, leadership matters. Companies with better leaders will outperform those with less qualified leaders. We often see this in the rear view mirror as we diagnose what went wrong after a company has failed. How then can we anticipate what makes effective leaders so that we can recommend in advance what leaders should know and do?

One challenge with defining what makes effective leaders is that the leadership field is littered with hundreds and thousands of models, ideas, frameworks, tools and approaches.

If we Google the word "leader," we get more than 300 million hits. On Amazon, there are over 500,000 books that have to do with leaders as the topic. There is enormous concept clutter around what leadership means and how to improve it.

Hence, it is no wonder that when any roomful of leaders or potential leaders are asked what effective leaders need to be, know or do, there are as many answers as there are people in the room. Leaders are authentic, have judgment and emotional intelligence, practice the 7 Habits and know the 21 Irrefutable Laws. They are like Lincoln, Moses, Jack Welch, Santa Claus, Mother Teresa, Jesus, Mohammed and Attila the Hun. So as Asian companies work to build more effective leaders, it is important to start by simplifying and synthesizing a clear sense of effective leadership rather than generating more complexity and confusion.

In this chapter, I want to share our last decade of thinking and research on how to answer the question "What is an effective leader?" and to apply that answer to the Asian context.

The Leadership Code

Defining effective leadership calls for a unique research methodology. To determine the degree to which effective leaders had common or different skills and an identification of those skills required information from those who had exposure to thousands of leaders. Traditional large-scale surveys of many leaders would not work because these individual respondents would only know about their specific situation and not have an overview of the overall leadership landscape. To answer our questions, Norm Smallwood, Kate Sweetman and I deployed a key informant methodology. We identified leadership experts who crafted leadership theory and had studied leaders across organizations, industries and countries. These expert key informants have done extensive research and practice on Leadership 360's to assess leaders, conduct coaching engagements to develop leaders and consulting assignments to build leadership architectures.

These experts also needed to have synthesized their vast experiences into books and articles where they presented their point of view about what makes good leadership. While our sample of 15 thought leaders may be small, it is a large percentage of the leadership expert population who met our key informant criteria. They are the "thought leaders" of this field.[2] Then, we proceeded to ask them to do a qualitative meta-analysis of their work. Traditional meta-analyses synthesize the findings of empirical studies to draw broad general conclusions. In this case, no one has studied the questions we were pursuing, so we asked the experts to each perform a qualitative meta-analysis on their work and to tell us the extent to which they felt leaders had common versus different skills. This key informant, qualitative meta-analysis is the right methodo-logy for the questions we asked. Our research is not about what 15 respondents think but about what millions of leaders think as filtered by those who shape and study their thinking. We are also pleased with the reliability of these 15 key experts since their results converge.

We believe that our results can be further tested and refined but that they are directionally correct. Perhaps the best confirmation is that when we have shared our conclusion of the five basic rules that leaders must follow and presented the five rules, we have had consistent confirmation of both findings. (The best proof of this is when we presented the five rules that leaders must follow and our conclusion based on these rules, we received consistent confirmation of both findings from our respondents.) The original 15 experts and now thousands of people to whom we have presented these findings have validated them.

In our discussions with these thought leaders, we focused on two simple but elusive questions:

1. What percentage of effective leadership is basically the same? Are there some common rules that any leader anywhere must adhere to? Is there a recognizable Leadership Code?

2. If there are common rules that all leaders must follow, what are they?

To the first question, the experts varied as they estimated that somewhere in the range of 50 to 85 percent of leadership characteristics are shared across all effective leaders. The range is fairly broad, to be sure, but consistent. As one of our interviewees put it: "I think . . . that 85 percent of the competencies in various competency models appear to be the same. I think we have a relatively good handle on the necessary competencies for a leader to possess in order to be effective." Then the expert added something of equally great significance: "But there are some other variables that competency models do not account for. [Among] the variables that I think we don't account for include . . . the leader's personal situation (family pressures, economics, competition, social, etc.); internal influences such as health, energy, vitality and resilience; the intensity of effort the individual is willing to put forth; ambition and drive, as well as the willingness to sacrifice."[3]

Answers like these encouraged us to develop an integrated framework. From the body of interviews we conducted, we concluded that 60 to 70 percent of leadership effectiveness would be contained in a Leadership Code if we could crack it. Synthesizing the data, the interviews and our own research and experience, a framework emerged that we simply call the Leadership Code.

An analogy guided our thinking. How different is a luxury Lexus sedan from a Toyota minivan? If you are like most people, you likely view the two vehicles as being very different from each other, perhaps even opposites. The Lexus appeals to people interested in comfort and prestige while driving around. The family friendly minivan, on the other hand, is a perfect vehicle for an active family on a budget. You may love to drive either one and not want to be caught dead in the other, believing them to be very different species.

But are they really? Underneath the obvious external characteristics, they share more in common than they differ. First of all, both of them are forms of individual (versus mass) transportation. They both get you where you need to go. They each do that by sharing an important set of core elements: drive train, crankshaft, engine, brakes, wipers, blades and batteries. In fact, when you add them up, the degree to which any two cars share fundamental similarities is much greater than their differences.

As we listened to leadership experts, we felt that the same logic would apply. Does an effective leader at, say, Panasonic in any way resemble an effective leader at Lenovo? Does an effective leader in a bootstrapping POE in any way resemble an effective leader at the more bureaucratic SOE? Does an effective leader in an emerging market (e.g., Vietnam) resemble an effective leader in a more mature market (e.g., Singapore)?

In an effort to create a useful visual, we have mapped out two dimensions (Time and Focus) and placed what we have labelled as Personal Proficiency (self management) at the center as an underlying support for the other two. Figure 2.1 synthesizes the Leadership Code and captures the five rules of leadership that embody leadership DNA.

FIGURE 2-1. THE LEADERSHIP CODE

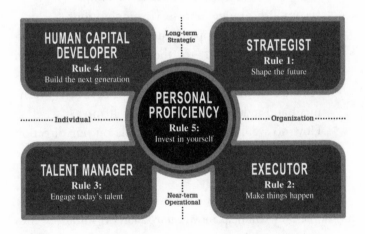

Rule 1: Shape the future. This rule is embodied in the Strategist dimension of the leader. Strategists answer the question "Where are we going?" and make sure that those

around them understand the direction as well. They not only envision but also can create a future. They figure out where the organization needs to go to succeed, they test these ideas pragmatically against current resources (money, people, organizational capabilities), and they work with others to figure out how to get from the present to the desired future. Strategists have a point of view about the future and are able to position their organization to create and respond to that future. The rules for strategists are about creating, defining and delivering principles of what can be.

Strategists in the Asian context must be aware of business conditions that affect their organization and deal with some of the following questions:

- How do we grow our business outside our home country to become a regional and global player?
- How do we continue to create a unique ability to accomplish product and service innovation?
- How do we anticipate future customer expectations and respond to them more quickly than competitors?
- How do we manage the connections between government and industry as we grow our firm?
- How do we create a shared agenda on our direction and engage employees in personalizing our corporate strategy?

As leaders at all levels work on these (and other) strategic questions, they will help move their Asian organizations into new markets, products, services and strategic spaces that enable them to compete.

Rule 2: Make things happen. Turn what you know into what you do. The Executor dimension of the leader focuses on the question "How will we make sure we get to where we are going?" Executors translate strategy into action. Executors understand how to make change happy, to assign accountability, to know which key decisions to take and which to delegate, and to make sure that teams work well together. They keep promises to multiple stakeholders. Executors make things happen, and put the systems in place for others to do the same. The rules for executors revolve around disciplines for getting things done and the technical expertise to get the right things done right.

Executors in the Asian context must build organizations that are known for their agility, discipline and responsiveness. They must deal with questions such as:

- How do we build our organization's ability to respond quickly to changing business conditions?
- How do we ensure clear accountability for results within the Asian culture of collaboration?
- How do we identify, measure and track organization results?
- How do we ensure discipline in reengineering and improving our processes?

As leaders in Asian firms focus on execution, they turn general intentions into measurable actions.

Rule 3: Engage today's talent. Leaders who optimize talent today answer the question "Who goes with us on our business journey?" Talent Managers know how to identify, build and engage talent to get results now. Talent Managers identify what skills are required, draw talent to their organizations, engage them, communicate extensively and ensure that employees turn in their best efforts. Talent Managers generate intense personal, professional and organizational loyalty. The rules for Talent Managers center around resolutions that help people develop themselves for the good of the organization.

Talent managers in the Asian context help communicate and motivate current talent. In the Asian context, some unique questions include:

- How do we help Asian employees have the competencies required to help companies reach their goals?
- How do we help Asian managers become professional leaders?
- How do we engage today's employees to continue to give discretionary energy to work while managing increased interest in work/life balance?
- How do we help employees find meaning in the work that they do?

Asian leaders who deal with these questions will ensure that Asian employees are competent (being able to do their work), committed (willing to do their work), and feel a sense of contribution (finding meaning from doing their work).

Rule 4: Build the next generation. Leaders who are Human Capital Developers answer the question, "Who stays and sustains the organization for the next generation?" Talent Managers ensure shorter-term results through people while Human Capital Developers ensure that the organization has the longer-term competencies required for future strategic success. Just as good parents invest in helping their children succeed, Human Capital Developers help future leaders be successful. Human Capital Developers throughout the organization build a workforce plan focused on future talent, understand how to develop the future talent and help employees see their future careers within the company.

Human Capital Developers ensure that the organization will outlive any single individual. Human Capital Developers implement rules that demonstrate a pledge to building the next generation of talent.

Human Capital Developers in the Asian context are concerned about next-generation Asian employees. They will deal with such questions as:

- What are the career development opportunities for our current employees?
- How do we source the employees in the future who will be fit for service?
- How do we prepare our more local Asian employees to be successful in the global context?
- How do we build an employee value proposition that attracts, retains and engages talented employees?
- How do we manage leadership succession so that the next generation of leaders are prepared for their challenges?

Asian leaders who deal with these questions will help develop their workforce for the challenges ahead.

Rule 5: Invest in yourself. At the heart of the Leadership Code—literally and figuratively—is Personal Proficiency. Effective leaders cannot be reduced to what they know and do. Who they are as human beings has everything to do with how much they can accomplish with and through other people. Leaders are learners: from success, failure, assignments, books, classes, people, and life itself. Passionate about their beliefs and interests, they expend an enormous personal energy and attention on whatever matters to them. Effective leaders inspire loyalty and goodwill in others because they themselves act with integrity and trust. Decisive and impassioned, they are capable of bold and courageous moves. Confident in their ability to deal with situations as they arise, they can tolerate ambiguity. Proficient leaders act out of a strong moral code that connects values to actions.

Asian leaders need to be personally proficient by taking care of themselves on a number of dimensions:

- Physical: Taking care of their bodies (nutrition, exercise, sleep) and space so that they are fit for service
- Emotional: Managing their identity, energy and passion so that they have resilience and stability
- Social: Ensuring both tight and loose ties with colleagues at work and friends outside of work so that they have a strong support network
- Intellectual: Having learning agility so that they can adapt to new circumstances
- Spiritual: Maintaining a strong sense of values so that they act with clear conscience and within the bounds of the societal moral code

When Asian leaders build their personal proficiency, they are able to turn their personal confidence into other support.

In the past few years, we have worked with these five rules of leadership. As we have done so, we can make some summary observations.

- All leaders must excel at Personal Proficiency. Without the foundation of trust and credibility, you cannot ask others to follow you. While individuals may have different styles (e.g., introvert versus extrovert, intuitive versus sensing), any individual leader must be seen as having personal proficiency to engage followers. This is probably the toughest of the five domains to train and some individuals are naturally more capable than others.

- All leaders must have one towering strength. Most successful leaders have at least one of the other four roles in which they excel. Most are personally predisposed to one of the four areas. These are the signature strengths of your leaders.
- All leaders must be at least average in his or her "weaker" leadership domains. It is possible to train someone to learn how to be strategic, execute, manage talent and develop future talent. There are behaviors and skills that can be identified, developed and mastered.
- The higher up in the organization that the leader rises, the more he or she needs to develop excellence in more than one of the four domains.

What Else Is Needed? Leadership Brand

We describe Leadership Code as a synthesis of what it takes to be an effective leader. According to our thought leaders, it also explains about 60 to 70 percent of the leadership puzzle. What about the other 30 to 40 percent?

To explain the latter, think of giving Richard Branson, CEO of Virgin Airlines, and Jeff Immelt, CEO of GE, a Leadership Code 360. We bet that both would score very high on the 360. Both are strong Strategists; they both know how to execute and get their ideas implemented by others; they are both high in Personal Proficiency; both are Talent Managers; and both are concerned about the next generation of talent and act as Human Capital Developers. Hence, according to our 360, they are both effective leaders.

FIGURE 2-2. THE LEADERSHIP BRAND

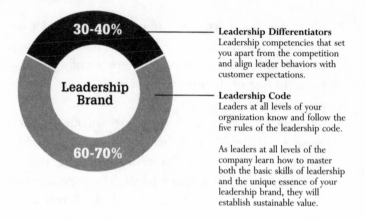

They have the Code competencies. But they are also very different, as Figure 2.2 will explain.

From a personal style perspective, Immelt tends to be more corporate-looking than Branson. He wears his hair shorter, is clean shaven and wears a suit and tie most of the time (we are not sure if we have ever seen the shaggy-haired Branson in a suit, much less with a tie). Branson is playful while Immelt tends to come across as more conservative and business-like. Immelt speaks in a more articulate manner and Branson tends to use "colorful" language to make his point. Branson seems more fun loving while Immelt seems more authoritative. So they have some differences in their style and perhaps some important other differences as leaders. But the Leadership Code 360 does not pick up what we call leader differentiators. So what are leader differentiators and how are they different from the fundamentals of the Leadership Code?

In our book, *Leadership Brand* (Ulrich and Smallwood, HBSP, 2007), we focused on these unique aspects of leadership. Our simple formula for Leadership Brand is comprised as follows:

$$\frac{\text{Leadership}}{\text{Code}} \times \frac{\text{Leadership}}{\text{Differentiators}} = \text{Leadership Brand}$$

Rather than derive leadership differentiators from interviews of successful and less successful leaders (a traditional approach in most competency models), we suggest that leadership differentiators for any organization may be derived from the firm's identity or *firm brand*. This firm brand is the way the company wants to be described by its target customers. Typically, the firm brand descriptors are the firm's customer value proposition along with how the company wants its target customers to experience that value proposition. Singapore Airlines' value proposition is outstanding service. Its commitment to quality customer care differentiates it from other airlines that may compete only on price. It works to ensure that its leaders will treat employees with the same dignity that it treats its customers. Defining leadership from the outside-in by starting with customer expectations ensures that leadership behavior inside a firm drives the customer experience.

With a clear identity in the mind of customers, the next step is to translate these firm brand descriptors into unique leadership differentiators. These leadership differentiators are the unique leadership competencies that make the firm brand real to the customers whenever they interact with any employee of the firm. These leadership differentiators are always outside-in; they bring the customer mindset to the table. In the Singapore Airlines example, the best Singapore Airlines leaders make sure that whenever a customer flies on a Singapore Airlines flight, he or she would have an exceptional experience.

Let us revisit Immelt and Branson. Jeff Immelt personifies GE's firm identity. He is a role model to other GE leaders about how the firm should be seen by outside stakeholders. GE's firm identity is about organic growth and innovation with a lot of measurement and accountability going on. Virgin's firm identity is about fun, irreverence, challenging the status quo and that is exactly what Richard Branson is constantly doing. He lives on an island and seems to enjoy the high life in ways that the rest of us can only dream of. He personifies the leadership style of the Virgin brand.

When GE or Virgin or Southwest can develop leaders at every level who have their own style that fits within the context of the differing firm identities, the company has a leadership brand that is appreciated by customers and employees and rewarded by financial markets as an envied capability.

For Asian leaders to build the leadership brand of their organizations, they need to start from the outside-in. They need to identify their target customers who are the largest customers in their industry. For Singapore Airlines, these are frequent business travelers who spend more on travel. They need to figure out what these travelers want the most from a supplier. In Singapore Airlines, business travelers care about being on time, having hassle-free check-in service and an exceptional in-flight experience (seat, food, entertainment). They then need to identify leadership behaviors of leaders at all levels that will ensure these customer expectations. These leaders at the corporate level who do scheduling, in the airport who manage check in, and on the aircraft who deal with passengers, are all trained to provide targeted customers with an exceptional experience. These desired leadership behaviors are then woven into the HR practices (hiring the right people, training them to do the right things, paying them for doing them right, and communicating to them the importance of what and how to act). Singapore Airlines' HR practices match customer expectations. When the activities inside an organization reflect the expectations of customers outside the organization, a brand has been created. This is summarized in Figure 2.3.

FIGURE 2-3. LOGIC FOR LEADERSHIP BRAND

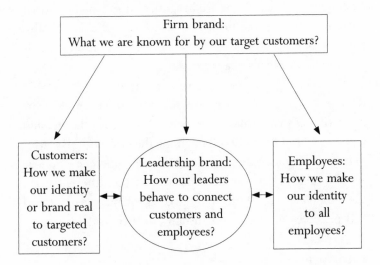

When Asian leaders become more focused on customers, they can then build leaders whose behaviors are consistent with those customer expectations. This is counter to some Asian operations that begin with building internal efficiency and operational excellence. When leaders throughout an organization act consistently with customer expectations, then employees will begin to not only understand but appreciate how their day-to-day actions build customer value.

Conclusion

It is not about Leadership Code versus Leadership Differentiators. It is about building leaders who have both. Leaders need to have the Leadership Code building blocks to be effective leaders and they need to know how their organization is unique in how it delivers on the desired customer connection. Effective leaders know and do the fundamentals of the Leadership Code and also know and do the Leadership Differentiators that ensure that each customer is assured the right experience whenever that customer touches the firm. It is not easy to be an effective leader but getting clarity amidst all of the confusing signals about what it entails is a good start.

In Asian organizations where most agree that leadership deficits will hinder future growth, it is important to start by clarifying what makes an effective leader. The Leadership Code and Leadership Brand might be the basis for this clarity. When companies build their leadership competency models, they should include both the basics and the differentiators, then they can create an integrated set of management and HR practices to create and sustain effective leadership.

Endnotes

1. The ideas in this chapter have been developed with Norm Smallwood and Kate Sweetman.
2. These generous thought leaders included: Jim Bolt (leadership development efforts); Richard Boyatzis (competency models and resonant leadership); Jay Conger (leadership skills relating to strategy); Bob Fulmer (leadership skills); Bob Eichinger (works with Mike Lombardo to extend work from Center for Creative Leadership; leadership abilities); Marc Effron (large studies of global leaders); Marshall Goldsmith (development of global leadership

skills); Gary Hamel (leadership relating to strategy); Linda Hill (how managers become leaders; leadership in emerging economies); Jon Katzenbach (leaders from within the organization); Jim Kouzes (how leaders build credibility); Morgan McCall (represents Center for Creative Leadership); Barry Posner (how leaders build credibility); Jack Zenger and Joe Folkman (how leaders deliver results and become extraordinary).

3. Personal correspondence with Jack Zenger.

CHAPTER 3

Developing Asia's Corporate Leadership
Challenges and Moving Forward

Wee Chow Hou

There are many challenges facing the development of corporate leaders and leadership within Asia. For Asian companies that are increasingly operating in the global arena, there is the added challenge of developing corporate leaders who can excel in the global arena. Are Asian corporate leaders ready? How can Asian companies better prepare their leaders and managers?

Introduction

For the last several decades, many Asian governments and companies have sent their senior executives to the best business schools like Harvard, Stanford and INSEAD for advanced management programs. Thousands of top Asian students are also sent to the best universities in North America and Europe for university and postgraduate education in various fields. Such a phenomenon is not at all surprising considering the dominance of Western multinational corporations (MNCs). Many of these MNCs have invested heavily in Asia and are largely responsible for the creation of jobs and the transfer of technology and management knowledge.

Take the case of Singapore. Since its independence in 1965, its economy has been fueled by Western MNCs. To learn more from the West, many of its public and private sector officials have been schooled in the very best universities in the West. This trend continues till even today. Certainly, Singapore is not the exception, but rather represents the norm among Asian countries. Since China opened up to the world in 1978, the number of Chinese who have left to study in America, Europe and Australia easily run into several hundred thousands. Today, the Chinese government have also begun to send their civil servants for learning overseas.

In recent years, however, a new trend is emerging. Spearheaded by China,[1] more and more Asian companies are now beginning to exert their business and economic presence in the world. With the weakening of Western economies arising from the 2008–09 financial tsunami and the collapse of many financial and other corporations, Asian companies are likely to make greater forays into the West. Their increased presence may include increased investments, and more significantly, through mergers and acquisitions. Already, many business analysts and scholars are forecasting that Asian companies will increasingly be ranked among *Fortune* Global 500 companies, and the number may cross the 100 mark within the next 20 to 30 years.

Along with the increasing presence of Asian companies in the global scene, a logical question to ask is whether they are ready to become true MNCs. By this, I mean not only buying over companies from other countries, but also having the ability to run them well and be in the position to transfer management know-how and technology, and to groom talent, like what Western MNCs have been doing for decades.

Challenges Facing Development of Corporate Leadership in Asia

There are many challenges facing the development of corporate leaders and leadership within Asia. What I would like to highlight are the additional challenges for Asian corporate leaders in Asian companies who are attempting to go abroad and operate in the global arena.

Readiness of Asian Corporate Leadership

Before venturing into the world, Asian corporate leaders need to address a fundamental question—are they ready for the challenge? By this, I do not mean having adequate financial resources. No doubt, many Asian companies have deep pockets today and buying up foreign companies, especially in the current depressed markets, is the least of problems. What I am referring to is the ability of Asian CEOs to manage overseas operations and foreign talents, especially those from the West. In other words, do they have the expertise and experience, communication skills and knowledge to operate in complicated regulatory environments, and the adaptiveness and shrewdness to handle the media, analysts, unions and lobbyists? Beyond all these lie the issues of psychology and confidence—do they have the right mindset and psyche to excel in the highly competitive and often combative and hostile business environment of the West?

The experiences of Chinese companies thus far have not been very favorable. Their acquisition experiences of American and European companies have been disastrous. Singapore, which I view as being ahead of the curve, also does not have a spectacular record. It has, from time to time, encountered severe obstacles, even among neighboring countries such as Malaysia, Thailand and Indonesia.

Can training solve this problem? How can we prepare potential Asian corporate leaders who are competent, ready and comfortable to run overseas companies?

Readiness for Asian Corporate Leadership

Even as Asian corporate leaders are ready to take on the challenge, is the world ready for them? This is a more intriguing question. Historically, many Asian countries were colonies of Western empires like the British, the Dutch and the French. The colonial past has created a double whammy effect—an inevitable inferiority complex among Asians and on the reverse, a superiority complex among the former Western colonial masters. In fact, the former, to some extent, has also affected the readiness and psyche of Asian corporate leaders in terms of their ability to operate in the terrain of their former colonial masters.

The latter—a hangover superiority complex that dates back to the colonial days—may impact the willingness of Westerners to work under Asian CEOs and management. Asian companies may think they are ready and have all the necessary traits to do well in the Western world. However, if the Western world is not ready to accept Asian bosses on their home ground, success stories remain to be tested.[2] Without doubt, historical and political baggage, cultural differences, values, attitudes and behavior, and social nuances can become severe hindrances in accepting another country's presence, more so if that country has not been doing well in the past or when the relationships have not been strong historically.[3] In fact, this legacy "complex" is likely to continue for the next 20 to 30 years. To me, it will only be overcome gradually when Asian countries and their companies continue to do well globally and when the Westerners realize that they cannot do without the presence of Asian investments, and along with them, Asian bosses.

Continued Relevance of Western MNCs and Institutions

In view of the massive growth of Asian companies, a pertinent question to raise is whether Western institutions and MNCs are suitably qualified to train Asian corporate leaders to run Asian companies? My argument is that leadership principles are universal, but the practice of the same principles may be greatly affected by culture, politics and social nuances. For example, the relative differences in emphasis on *guanxi* versus contracts, long-term versus short-term returns, trust and loyalty versus meritocracy, people versus tasks, team versus individual performances, flexibility versus adherence to rules, and others are clearly demonstrated when MNCs operate in Asia. The reverse will be true for Asian companies aspiring to operate in the West.

There are also different orientations and focus when it comes to judging what corporate leaders and leadership should be. If you read Chinese classics such as those by

Confucius and Lao Zi, you will observe that they focus on the person, the values and the character of the leader. This is totally different in the West, where you talk about effective habits of CEOs, what CEOs should do, and so on. They tend to focus on the functions, tasks and responsibilities. In the past, much of such Western practices, including the need for good corporate governance, controls and transparency, have been repeatedly inculcated into Asian managers working for the MNCs. Western critics have also not restrained themselves in their criticism of the Asian way of managing companies. Indeed, during the last Asian financial crisis in 1997, the criticisms came fast and harsh, with some even advocating that Asian companies deserved to "die."

Ironically, barely 12 years later, the same "preachers" of transparency and corporate governance have been found guilty of greed, frauds, scandals and massive cheating. Wall Street was almost brought to its knees and the global financial tsunami that followed caused damages that were several hundred times more disastrous! What can be learned from this episode? It is not the sound structures, systems, processes and controls that caused the catastrophe. It is the lack of integrity, moral values and character among corporate leaders that caused the disaster. Amazingly, some of them still do not feel that what they did was wrong, and some even took the U.S. federal bailout money to further enrich themselves with bonuses.

In the light of what has happened, it would be worth reflecting on whether the Western model of picking, training, grooming and rewarding corporate leaders, and the Western model of management will increasingly be challenged. If so, how then should Asian corporate leaders and leadership be developed and trained? In the past, this issue was not pressing at all. However, as Asian companies begin to flex their business muscles internationally, they do need to address this matter head-on.

Board of Directors in Asian Companies

Another concern that should bother Asian companies desiring to go global is that of training and upgrading the quality of the board members. Without doubt, the Board of Directors represents the apex of corporate leadership and is tasked with charting the strategic directions of the company, including major investments, overseas expansion, mergers and acquisitions, and even the hiring and firing of top executives, especially the CEO. They can either facilitate or stifle the global expansion plans of companies. For example, if the board does not have a global orientation and is not confident to move into the riskier international arena, how can the CEO go out there to cut deals and carry out mergers and acquisitions?

Regretfully, most corporate board members in many Asian companies lack the global exposure and experience. Many are not former CEOs of companies nor have they managed business enterprises before. In many countries such as China, board members are often made up of former cabinet ministers, top civil servants and bureaucrats.[4] Of course, leveraging on private sector top executives and professionals, and attracting overseas directors is one way to go. However, it is only a partial solution. Certainly, for Asian companies to effectively exert their presence globally, upgrading the quality of corporate boards has to be among the top agenda.[5]

Moving Forward

Moving forward, I would like to raise several points for consideration.

Leveraging on Foreign Talents

As mentioned earlier, there is an urgency to train more Asian corporate leaders. It would be a very slow and difficult process to source and groom corporate leaders within Asia, given the severe shortage of talents. A viable and necessary alternative is to supplement the pool by recruiting foreign talents. This will accelerate the globalization process, shorten the learning curve of Asian companies, expand the talent pool and reduce the tuition fees. The challenge is to decide on what kind of foreign talents are needed, and the willingness to pay world-class salaries. This, of course, can create unevenness in the system, and at times, social tension. Take the case of Singapore. We have been successful in recruiting some world-class corporate talents at world-class salaries. However, they are not necessarily running the best and most profitable companies in Singapore. Meanwhile, some element of envy and jealousy may arise from other sectors of the population.

There is another important consideration in recruiting foreign talents. The search process must be very detailed and thorough. The focus should not be on their track records and skills alone. In the context of Asia, they must be leaders of high moral character and integrity, and who can identify themselves with Asia. There must be in-depth sensitization and orientation programs in place to educate them to understand nuances of Asian politics, culture, social norms, business practices and other aspects. The ultimate success of employing highly talented foreign top executives must be that they are able to bring Asian companies to greater heights and horizons. Better yet, some of them may even opt to stay for good. If they merely come and go and behave like professional nomads, then such a scheme will have little value.[6]

Institute for Asian Corporate Leadership Development

It has been mentioned that MNCs and Western institutions may not be the best outfits to train and groom Asian corporate leaders. This is where setting up an institute for Asian corporate leadership development, say, within Singapore, may be worth considering. Currently, within Singapore, corporate leadership training is carried out by various companies and institutions in very haphazard and fragmented ways.[7] There is, simply put, a lack of focus, and efforts are very much opportunity-driven. It is timely to set up a national-level institute that is tasked to carry out this function in a more holistic and strategic manner by harnessing all available resources locally, regionally and internationally.

This institute, among other functions, can look into the following areas:

1. To research and develop the course contents, cases and materials that are relevant for training and developing Asian corporate leaders.
2. To have the capabilities to customize training programs according to where the CEO will be operating. For example, the approach for leading and managing companies in less developed economies like Africa can be very different from that of operating in Europe or America.

3. To integrate the best of East and West approaches for the development of Asian corporate leaders by working with the best regional and international partners. Despite some reservations expressed, there are still many lessons that Asia can learn from Western institutions and corporations.

4. To act as a regular platform for Asian CEOs and corporate leaders to share ideas and experiences. This will enable a more systematic pooling of shared knowledge and expertise and act as a net-worked organization and conduit for the advance-ment of knowledge and information exchange for corporate leaders.

5. To create a mentoring-coaching scheme whereby young and promising corporate executives can be personally tutored under the wings of the established Asian CEOs.[8] This is like an apprenticeship scheme to expose them to the highest level of corporate decision-making.

6. To provide other forms of exposure and training that help build the moral character and values of Asian corporate leaders.

Deciding on the Theater of Operation

Finally, something that is often overlooked is the prioritization of the type of corporate leaders needed in Asia. First, we need to define and identify the theater of operations for Asian companies. Where (which markets and regions) can Asian companies best excel in? Is it in the less well-developed economies, within other Asian economies, or in Europe or America? Clearly, the approaches to be taken to do well in one country or region can be significantly different from those in other places. In other words, there is no one-size-fits-all leadership style or behavior in managing overseas operations.

Take the case of China. Other than direct exporting, many of their overseas direct investments and acquisitions in Europe and America have been met with very severe challenges, and in a number of prominent cases, failures. The Chinese problem is what I have raised earlier. Are Chinese companies ready to manage Western companies and operate in Western societies? Are these Western companies and Westerners ready to work under Chinese bosses? My answer to both questions is a definite "no." What then would be a better option? Interestingly, Chinese companies are doing very well in Africa and in the less-developed world today—areas where they are much welcomed and needed and where they can be the "big brother."

Singapore, too, paid "high tuition fees" in its early days of going overseas. It was not that Singaporean companies were not ready. Rather, it was the economies that we went into that were not ready for us. Today, we realign and readjust our strategies, and we are beginning to see very positive results.

In sum, Asian companies must first determine their theaters of operation. This, in turn, will affect the kind of talents they should recruit, the kind of training to be provided, and the kind of corporate leaders to be groomed. In other words, the training of Asian corporate leaders cannot be carried out in a vacuum. A more systematic and strategic kind of approach in developing human resource policies, career placement and development will have to be instituted. Only in this way can Asian companies be more successful globally.

Conclusion

For Asian companies expanding into the global arena, the challenge of developing corporate leaders is of paramount importance. There is no one-size-fits-all solution. We should not blindly copy from the West, nor should we stubbornly stick to the Eastern way. What we need is to learn from what works best in both systems and understand why they work. Take the Singapore model for example. Singapore survived largely because of its ability to integrate the best from both the East and West. Singapore's economy is built largely on Western technology, management practices and legal systems, and heavily dependent on MNCs. Yet, the society is heavily grounded in Asian values. Look at Singapore's Minister Mentor, Mr. Lee Kuan Yew. Although educated in English and having a university education in Cambridge, he is very Asian, very Chinese, very Confucian in his values. He has left behind a legacy for governing Singapore—an integration of the best of the East and West.

I would like to conclude with my favorite saying about developing Asian corporate leaders and leadership: "The answer is in our hands" and only Asians can resolve it in the most effective way.

Endnotes

1. Prior to the emergence of China, Japan and Korea are the only two Asian countries that have companies exerting some noticeable influences in the world through their conglomerates known as *kereitsu, zaibatsu* and *chaebol*.

2. Interestingly, when the author raised this point several years ago in one of his speaking engagements to a Japanese conglomerate, its Chairman could not help but share his company's experiences in operating globally. According to him,

his group had done very well in many countries, especially in Asia and other developing economies. However, in the United States and in parts of Europe, his group suffered repeated setbacks. His conclusion—many Americans and Europeans were not ready to work with the Japanese as their bosses. After all, the Japanese lost World War II to the United States and the former NATO countries and Japan had to be rebuilt with much foreign aid from the West.

3. In the case of Singapore, this challenge even extends to investments and acquisitions of companies in its neighboring countries.

4. In the case of Temasek-linked companies in Singapore, the move to internationalize board members was only instituted about 15 years ago. This, however, is not commonly practiced outside the Temasek-linked com-panies. In China, there have been some very modest attempts to invite overseas experts to sit on the boards of state-owned enterprises in recent years.

5. China, for sure, has recognized this serious problem. It has increasingly sent the Board of Directors and top executives of its state-owned enterprises overseas for training and exposures.

6. Interestingly, Singapore originated from an immigrant society. Today, this policy of welcoming foreign talents remains. Many high-caliber foreign professionals have come to work here and a good number have opted to make Singapore their home. In fact, even within the Singapore Parliament and among corporate bigwigs, we still have members who are first-generation Singaporeans.

7. For example, CapitaLand's CLIMB (CapitaLand Institute of Management and Business) and Temasek Holdings' BLC (Business Leadership Centre) offer leadership-related courses to their "in-house" clients, while local universities like NTU, NUS and SMU and foreign schools located in Singapore, like INSEAD, Chicago, ESSEC, all offer various kinds of management and leadership courses.

8. They could be appointed as personal assistants to the CEOs.

CHAPTER 4

Winning the Talent War in China Through Unique Value Propositions

Arthur Yeung

The twenty-first century is a century for Asia. As many economists predict that Asian countries like China and India will emerge to be one of the largest world economies by the middle of this century, Asia presents tremendous growth opportunities for both Western multinational firms and Asian local firms. While many companies can quickly discover that there is no lack of market opportunities, capital supply or low-cost manual labor in Asia, high-caliber talent and globally oriented business leaders remain scarce resources and impediment to growth in the region. The severity of talent shortage varies substantially in different countries. China, for example, presents one of the extreme cases where demand for high-caliber talent far exceeds supply while talent shortage in other mature regions like Taiwan, Singapore and Hong Kong are much less challenging. This article presents findings of a recent study of seven Best Employers[1] in China which examines how these Best Employers differentiate themselves from other companies in their talent management approaches. The article will also suggest how companies can sharpen their effectiveness in talent management through a four-step process. While the article focuses primarily on the talent management challenges and strategies in China, I believe that the talent management philosophy and strategies discussed here should also be applicable to firms in other Asian economies facing serious imbalance in talent demand and supply.

Talent Challenges in China and Background of the Study

Fueled by an average annual GDP growth of 9.8 percent in the last 30 years (i.e., from 1979 to 2007), China has become one of the most attractive destinations for foreign direct investment (FDI),[2] attracting up to US$766 billion between 1980 and 2007 (Ministry of Commerce PRC, 2008).[3] In 2008 alone, US$108 billion of FDI was funneled into China's economy (Ministry of Commerce PRC, 2009),[4] with more than 60 MNCs relocating or establishing their Asia-Pacific regional headquarters in China (Yang, 2005).[5] In addition to establishing offshore manufacturing plants and local sales operations, more and more MNCs are setting up higher value-added business activities like global or regional R&D and logistic centers in China (over 400 regional R&D centers by 2005), requiring more sophisticated talent to run such operations. Meanwhile, local Chinese firms like Lenovo, Haier, Huawei, ZTE and TCL are pursuing rapid growth not only domestically but also in global markets. Also, many state-owned giants such as China Mobile, ICBC, CNOOC, SINOPEC, China Telecom and China Insurance in various industry sectors are being restructured to heighten their business competitiveness. The implication for all these business trends on human resource management is simple: China needs much more high-caliber talent and global managers to support business growth locally and internationally.

Unfortunately, due to the relative short history of a market-driven economy in China, the nation has a limited inventory of talent capable of leading and growing increasingly complex business operations. A recent McKinsey study (Farrell & Grant, 2005)[6] estimates that in the next 10 to 15 years, China will need approximately 75,000 globally competent managers to meet business requirements. But the reality is that China currently only has about 3,000 to 5,000 of such high-caliber managers. The study also points out that due to the gap between Chinese educational systems and corporate talent requirements, only one out of 10 university graduates in China is prepared to work for multinational firms because of inadequate language, computer and other skills. Obviously, the pipeline to the talent market is not well tuned, either.

The consequences created by the imbalance between demand and supply in talent are clearly felt among business leaders in China. Our recent interviews with over 20 CEOs from leading MNCs (including Coca-Cola, Kodak, Philips, Johnson & Johnson, Bayer, Unilever and Sony) in China revealed that talent management is the most frequently and consistently mentioned critical business issue (ahead of issues such as business model innovation, relationship with headquarters and supply chain management) that affects their ability to execute aggressive growth targets. With strong resource commitment and expectations from headquarters to grow the China market by two or three times in the next five years, these CEOs realize that talent, not technology or capital, is their most critical constraint to growth. Frequently highlighted talent management challenges include:

- How to recruit talent in areas of great shortage?
- How to retain critical talent?
- How to develop talent to compete in China and eventually support regional and global business needs?
- How to localize talent to succeed expatriates?
- How to energize and engage talent to increase their contribution to their jobs?

To understand how firms can be more effective in attracting, retaining, developing and engaging their talent to support their growth and success in China, we decided to benchmark some Best Employers and examine how these companies effectively manage their talent in spite of fierce competition in China. After sending out invitations to 30 Best Employers in China that were recently elected by Hewitt Associates (Bennett & Bell, 2004),[7] Watson Wyatt/Fortune (Watson Wyatt/*Fortune China*, 2005),[8] and China Central Television (CCTV), seven Best Employers agreed to participate in the study, representing a response rate of 23 percent. For each company that agreed to participate in the study, we conducted background research through publicly available information and then spent one day on site to understand the firm's talent management strategies by interviewing its CEO, HR leader, and seven to eight employees from different departments and levels in a focus group setting. We believe a triangulating approach from three different perspectives (business leader, HR and employees) is necessary to help us develop a more balanced and complete view of the talent management approach of these Best Employers.

Table 4.1 provides a company summary of the seven participating Best Employers which are diverse in terms

TABLE 4-1. BEST EMPLOYERS' PROFILES

	Business Field	Company Overview
Alibaba.com	E-commerce trading platform and service	↳ Founder: Jack Ma and 17 others ↳ Ranked No. 1 online B2B global trading marketplace for SMEs ↳ Achieved 100% growth in the last three years, reaching US$440 million in revenue with 10,000 employees
Bosera Fund Management	Mutual fund investment service for institutional and individual investors	↳ Founder: Xiao Feng ↳ Consistently ranked No. 1 or No. 2 fund management company in China ↳ Manages assets of RMB178 billion in 2008, 250 employees generated annual revenue of RMB2.35 billion
Li-Ning	Sportswear products	↳ Founder: Li Ning ↳ China's largest sporting goods company ↳ Grew around 40% in the last three years, reaching RMB6.7 billion sales revenue in 2008 with 4,000 employees
Mary Kay	Cosmetic and skin-care products through direct distribution	↳ President of Greater China: Paul Mak ↳ Most profitable Mary Kay subsidiary in the world and ranked No. 1 based on return on investment in China's cosmetic industry

TABLE 4-1. (continued)

	Business Field	Company Overview
Mary Kay		✦ Grew rapidly in recent years, reaching RMB4 billion sales revenue in 2008 with 700 employees and 400,000 independent beauty consultants
Portman Ritz-Carlton	5-star luxury hotel	✦ Founding General Manager: Mark DeCocinis ✦ Consistently ranked No. 1 among "Best Employers in Asia" and achieved highest employee satisfaction among 60 Ritz-Carlton hotels worldwide ✦ Manages 578 rooms with 700 employees, achieving year-on-year financial growth of 15%–18%
Shell	Energy exploration, production, and distribution	✦ Shell Exploration and Production CEO (China): Simon Durkin ✦ Ranked as one of the most respected companies in the world ✦ Shell E&P manages about 150 employees, plus 2,500 secondary and contract employees
Vanke	Real estate developer	✦ Founder: Wang Shi ✦ Ranked top real estate developer in China ✦ Grew at annual rate of 50% in the last three years, reaching RMB47.9 billion in 2008 with 16,500 employees

of industry (ranging from e-commerce, fund investment, sporting goods, cosmetic products, hotel service, energy and real estate development), employee size (160 to 15,000 full-time employees) and origin of ownership (three multinational firms and four local firms).

While all companies are to some extent wrestling with talent management challenges, we have found that these Best Employers are relatively more effective in attracting, retaining and engaging their targeted talent to achieve business success. This article summarizes our observations and reflections as to why these companies are so successful in this area. While the specific management practices of these Best Employers may vary substantially, their underlying people management philosophy and strategies are strikingly similar as follows:

(1) They manage talent based on the philosophy of "mutual investment"

(2) They develop and deliver differentiated talent management strategies based on unique value propositions

Talent Management Philosophy: "Mutual Investment"

All featured Best Employers have a strong and clear management philosophy on talent—they expect a lot from their talent and invest a lot to help them become successful. In other words, they "give" a lot and "get" a lot.

Through research and consulting experiences with hundreds of companies, I have found that different com-panies manage their people based on different philosophies. While such philosophies may not be explicitly articulated,

TABLE 4-2. PEOPLE MANAGEMENT PHILOSOPHIES

Expected Contribution
(What Companies "Get")

		Low/Narrow	High/Broad
Offered Inducement (What Companies "Give")	High/ Broad	Over Investment 1	Mutual Investment (organization-focused) 2
	Low/ Narrow	3 Economic Exchange (job-focused)	4 Under Investment

they can often be reflected in their people management decisions and practices. Based on the dimensions of what companies "give" (i.e., offered inducement to employees) and what companies "get" (i.e., expected contribution from employees), we can broadly categorize people management philosophies into four types (Tsui, A. & Wu, J., 2005),[9] as illustrated in Table 4.2.

"Economic exchange" means companies expect very little from employees in terms of their contribution and behavior. In return, employees do not expect much from the companies. It is purely an economic exchange—"You do your job and I pay your salary. We don't owe each other anything other than a job completed, and a fair wage paid." The classic forms of such relationships are contract workers or subcontractors.

"Under investment" means companies expect employees to work hard and contribute a lot to the company's success while offering relatively little in return (e.g., in terms of salary, benefits, job security, training, career development). Such relationships can be seen in firms that are facing fierce competition with razor-thin profit margins or those in a turnaround phase. Employees are asked to do more with less. For example, I know of a large retail chain in China that has grown 30 percent annually in the last three years, yet with zero percent increase in employee salaries. Such employment can last only for a while and is not sustainable.

"Over investment" means companies expect relatively little from employees but offer a lot in terms of salary increases, job security, reduced work hours, work environment, among other benefits. Such relationships can be seen in highly unionized settings (e.g., General Motors and Delphi) or state-owned enterprises. Employees feel entitled to regular raises and job security regardless of the overall performance of the companies. However, not many companies nowadays can afford such "luxury."

"Mutual investment" means companies expect employees to contribute a lot as people are their critical source of competitive advantage. Employees are not only expected to do their jobs better and faster over time, but also make broader contributions to the organization through employee suggestions, corporate taskforces, long-term commitment and the like. In return, companies offer employees a lot not only economically but socially and psychologically (e.g., long-term career development, abundant training opportunities, pleasant work environment, reasonable salary and benefits, close-knit social community, self-esteem and dignity). The Best Employers we studied such as the Portman Ritz-Carlton,

Mary Kay, Alibaba and Bosera all strongly demonstrate such people-focused management philosophy.

We believe the people management philosophy of a company is fundamental. Unless companies are willing to reexamine, challenge and revise their people management philosophy, it would be futile to simply benchmark the best practices from other innovative companies as such management practices will neither be rigorously implemented nor strictly adhered to, especially when companies are facing difficult times. In our interviews, we heard repeated stories about how business leaders showed genuine care towards employees, especially when the companies were facing tough business challenges. The following incidents clearly reflect the people management philosophy of such companies:

- In 1998, Mary Kay experienced its biggest crisis in China when the Chinese government issued a national ban on direct selling. Even though sales dropped to around RMB1 million a month, the company still kept the door open and did not lay off any staff. Instead, it asked for financial assistance from its headquarters during this tough time. In 2000, when Mary Kay decided to put all its order fulfilment process online, it needed to substantially reduce its staff in more than 50 beauty centers from an average of 20 to two. Many employees needed to be let go. However, before Mary Kay China launched this plan, the employees were fully informed about the changes, given the opportunity to transfer to the head office in Shanghai or a third-party company, and if, finally, they needed to be let go, the company provided them with fair and the best compensation within the policy regulations of the company. Due to the genuine care Mary Kay China showed to its employees, the employees reciprocated with their extraordinary effort. For example, employees at Nanjing beauty centers volunteered to work over-night until 6:00 A.M. on their last day of work so that all products could be ready for timely delivery by third-party logistics companies.

- In 2003, Portman Ritz-Carlton faced its lowest occupancy rate in history due to the SARS crisis. In April, its occupancy rate dropped drastically from 85 to 35 percent. While employees were concerned about the possible impact of such a crisis on their income and job security, the executive team responded by first taking a 30 percent pay cut and then asked everyone to work five days a week. In May, it got even worse and the occupancy rate was 17 to 18 percent. The leadership team further reduced the work week to four days and employees were asked to take their outstanding paid leave days. And when these reserves were getting used up, that was when everyone really pulled together. Employees who were single gave their shifts to colleagues who had families to support. During the whole crisis, the leadership team renewed employee contracts without a second thought. Some employees were worried that their contracts would not be renewed given the low occupancy rates, but the leaders reassured them if their performance and behavior were good, they would be retained. As a result, employee satisfaction rate that year was 99.9 percent.

Similar stories have been heard regarding how Jack Ma at Alibaba.com coped with a suspected SARS outbreak among its staff and how Xiao Feng at Bosera Fund Management dealt with a business crisis related to irregular trading practices by the company. All these leadership decisions speak louder than words and clearly convey how these companies treat their people with a long-term view and favor a win-win situation.

Differentiated Talent Management Strategy

If talent is critical to business success, the next question is how can companies attract, retain and engage their targeted talent better than other competitors in the talent market? Unique value proposition becomes critical. No matter what kind of competition companies are engaged in (for products, capital or talent), the only way that companies can out-compete others is to offer unique or superior values to their targeted stakeholders (customers, shareholders or talent) that their competitors cannot offer or offer so well. For companies that fail to differentiate themselves, the only way their stakeholders can judge them is purely financial in terms of price, dividend or salary.

As we interviewed the CEOs, HR leaders and employees of the Best Employers, we found that these companies differentiate and excel in competing for talent through specific themes or values that matter to their targeted talent on the one hand, and are critical to business success on the other. Instead of summarizing our findings of all seven Best Employers, we will describe in greater detail how two of the Best Employers manage to attract, retain, develop and engage their talent to deliver extraordinary business results.

Case No. 1: The Portman Ritz-Carlton

Excellent personalized guest services are critical to the Portman Ritz-Carlton in maintaining its reputation and achieving financial results. To consistently deliver high-quality personalized guest services, the Portman Ritz-Carlton understands that they need talent who can customize and satisfy customer needs in every customer interaction. How can the hotel attract, retain, develop and engage the right talent they need in a country where quality service is generally underdeveloped? The Portman Ritz-Carlton's unique value proposition to its targeted talent is simple and straightforward—"Setting our Ladies and Gentlemen up for success." The unique value proposition has three key elements and is delivered through a set of carefully aligned management practices:

- **Ladies and Gentlemen.** The Portman Ritz-Carlton treats its employees as Ladies and Gentlemen, which means treating them with respect and dignity. Such respect can be reflected through the various practices of how the hotel treats its employees. For example, all prospective employees regardless of their job positions will be personally interviewed by the General Manager; places where employees work and rest have the same standard as the public area which concretely portrays what "ladies and gentlemen serving ladies and gentlemen" means. In the service industry where employees are often mistreated with low self-esteem, the Portman Ritz-Carlton stands out in sharp contrast.

- **Setting up.** The Portman Ritz-Carlton provides employees with the right skills, empowerment and information support so that they are set up to do their jobs well (i.e., offering excellent and personalized services to their guests).

The Portman Ritz-Carlton provides training to employees to foster an understanding of company culture and improve their skills. Before new employees have any contact with guests, they receive a two-day orientation (called Gold Standard) on company culture and philosophy during which the General Manager and the executive team explain the Ritz-Carlton Credo, Employee Promise, and 20 Basics of Services. After that, they receive 30 days of training from a certified trainer from the department. In addition, every employee gets a minimum of 130 hours of training every year which involve training for their department, company culture, language and computer skills.

Employees are also fully empowered to comply with customer needs or to resolve customer complaints. One of Employee Basics states that "when a guest has a problem or needs something special you should break away from your regular duties, address and resolve the issue." Employees at the Portman Ritz-Carlton, like employees at any Ritz-Carlton hotel elsewhere, are empowered to spend up to US$2,000 to resolve customer complaints. And as long as there is a valid reason, there is no limit on the number of times employees can use that empowerment.

Through their numerous interaction with guests throughout their stay (e.g., check in, room service and housekeeping), employees continuously record guest preferences and needs in Guest Preference Forms. Every night, such preferences and needs are entered into the Ritz-Carlton's worldwide database ("Project Mystique") so whenever guests make a reservation at a Ritz-Carlton hotel, their needs and preferences are known and taken care of. When a guest has a complaint, employees are empowered not only to deal with the complaint immediately, but also to record the information on a "Guest Incident Action Form" and alert other departments of the incident so that appropriate action can be taken to recover customer satisfaction.

- **Success.** The Portman Ritz-Carlton offers employees a sense of achievement, pride, long-term career development opportunities (70 to 80 percent of leaders are promoted from within), and financial and non-financial reward through their work.

  Mark DeCocinis, the founding General Manager, believes that if you want your people to be the best, you must pay them top market salaries. While money is not the key motivator, employees are rewarded for improving the goals measured by guest satisfaction, financial performance and employee satisfaction at year end.

  Employees are rewarded and recognized for their outstanding customer service. Every quarter, a Five-Star Employee Award is granted; with the annual Award winner receiving a five-night stay for two at a Ritz-Carlton anywhere in the world, along with round-trip tickets for two and a US$500 allowance.

  Managers at the hotel know that their job is to motivate and recognize people. Employees are recognized at staff meetings and through the HR communication bulletin board. Employees also send first-class compliment cards to each other to recognize service excellence of their colleagues.

For businesses like the Portman Ritz-Carlton, where people are critical to its business success, the company expects a lot from their employees, yet it also invests a lot to induce and engage its targeted talent—not only economically but also psychologically and socially. This "mutual investment" philosophy is clearly the underlying employment relationship between the hotel and its employees. As we interviewed Mark DeCocinis and asked what contributed to the hotel's success in managing talent, his answer was simple and direct: "The secret is consistency in execution. Our priority is taking care of our people every day. We're in the service business and service comes only from people" (Yeung, 2006).[10] Because the employees are so critical to the hotel's success, the leadership team's foremost priority is to create an attractive work environment where the targeted talent of the hotel can be attracted, retained, developed and engaged through a set of aligned leadership behaviors and management practices.

Case No. 2: Alibaba.com

Similarly, for Alibaba.com to grow and succeed as an online trading marketplace, they need IT and sales professionals that build the company with strong entrepreneurship, innovation and service-orientation. To attract, retain and engage their targeted talent, Alibaba.com offers such unique value proposition: "A Smiling Community with a Dream." This unique value proposition also has three elements:

- **A Dream.** The dream to make a difference in how businesses are conducted over the Internet. The dream to collectively create and share wealth. Starting from the recruitment process, Jack Ma, the founder and CEO of Alibaba.com, always emphasizes to prospective candidates the importance to work for their own dreams, not the dream of the CEO or the company. The dream to revolutionize how trading is conducted around the world, the dream to build a firm that all Chinese can be proud of. Such a dream or mission has been continually reinforced and reminded by Ma over the years through various kinds of communication.

All employees of Alibaba.com receive stock options and in effect are owners of the organization. At Alibaba .com, stock options are not a tool for retention but for reward sharing. From five cents per share to five dollars per share in six years, many employees have not only shown tremendous pride in the company but also shared the fruits of their collective success for the well-being of both the society and themselves.

- **A Community.** Jack Ma offers a vivid image of the community where talent can enjoy working together to pursue their dream. Alibaba.com is a community with:
  - **blue sky** which means transparency in decision making and systems
  - **green forest** which means an environment conducive to innovative ideas
  - **solid ground** which means company decisions are financially and legally sound and solid
  - **free-flowing ocean** which means talents are free to rotate across businesses and functions
  - **harmonious residents** which means people share similar values and approaches in how they work together

  Communication is an important practice within Alibaba.com that helps maintain a culture of transparency. Employees have easy access to all executives, including Jack Ma, through the use of email, BBS and face-to-face meetings (monthly, quarterly or bi-annual staff meetings). Jack Ma sets a high standard for his executives to follow by regularly interacting with employees.

Strong shared values are essential in building a harmonious community where people feel comfortable working together and in ensuring that decisions and behaviors are aligned with company direction. Alibaba.com has gone the extra mile to make sure that people share the same values. When Alibaba .com hires people, they look for candidates with the same "smell"—people who are optimistic, happy, team oriented, hardworking and willing to invest their lives to achieve an ideal. When employees join the company, they attend at least ten days of orientation, focusing primarily on the company's vision, mission and values. When the company assesses the performance of employees, 50 percent is tied to values and 50 percent is tied to business results. When employees demonstrate behaviors contrary to company core values, they are asked to leave no matter how much income they generate or how senior a position they hold.

- **Smiling.** Alibaba.com carefully selects people who are optimistic, enjoy challenges and can turn stressful work into fun. As a matter of fact, the company logo is a smiling face.

  Alibaba.com creates an upbeat culture where people are challenged to take on "impossible" targets year after year. In 2002, the company goal was to break even. In 2003, the goal was to generate sales revenue of RMB1 million per day. In 2004, the goal was to make a profit of RMB1 million per day. In 2005, the goal was to contribute profit tax of RMB1 million per day. "Although the objectives each year seemed high and unreasonable, somehow we've always managed to accomplish those objectives. With past success we've built up the confidence to achieve the objectives, no matter what they are," says Lili Li, manager of the Sales Research Department.

For entrepreneurs like Jack Ma who have very little initial resources (e.g., financial capital, brand, intellectual property, customer relationship), talent is the only resource they can leverage to rapidly build a business to capture emerging business opportunities not only in China but also in the e-commerce industry. Such business leaders understand the importance of talent and they are willing to invest time and energy in nurturing and retaining the required talent. Similar to the Portman Ritz-Carlton hotel, Alibaba.com strongly practices the "mutual investment" philosophy. However, quite different from the Portman Ritz-Carlton Hotel, Alibaba.com attracts, retains, develops and engages its talent with a very different value proposition—"A Smiling Community with a Dream" due to the different needs and wants of its targeted talent.

Table 4.3 summarizes the unique value propositions of the Best Employers we studied. There are three similarities: (1) they focus on values that matter to both the top needs and wants of the targeted talent and the winning requirements of the company; (2) the differentiation is more than financial reward; (3) the unique value propositions are supported by key enabling practices.

TABLE 4-3. UNIQUE VALUE PROPOSITIONS OF BEST EMPLOYERS

Companies	Unique Value Propositions	Key Enabling Practices
Alibaba.com	A Smiling Community with a Dream	■ Attractive stock options ■ Value-based training and communication ■ Transparency in communication and decision making ■ Excitement and fun through stretch targets
Bosera Fund Management	Professional Excellence in a Caring and Supportive Organization	■ Invest in professional training and growth ■ Fair assessment system ■ IT support and enabling system ■ Pleasant work environment for employees
Li-Ning	Winning Globally Based on Sportsmanship	■ Reinforce mission and vision to create stretch for improvement ■ Select talent with professional expertise and passion for sports ■ Generous compensation to attract talent ■ Sports culture and lifestyle
Mary Kay	Enriching Women's Lives	■ Engage employees to pursue purposes of higher value ■ Character training that supports company's guiding principles ■ Reinforce and reward principle-based behaviors

Portman Ritz-Carlton	Setting Our Ladies and Gentlemen Up for Success	▪ Treat employees with dignity and respect ▪ Frequent communication and listening ▪ On-the-job and off-the-job training ▪ Empower employees to comply with guest needs or to resolve guest complaints ▪ Timely and relevant information support ▪ Financial and non-financial rewards
Shell	Company with Long-Term and Internationally Oriented Career Development Opportunities	▪ Selection based on potential, not professional, skills ▪ Systematic training with skills certification, business simulation, potential assessment ▪ Career development opportunities for international exposure and assignments
Vanke	Professional Growth in a Transparent and Ethical Organization	▪ Emphasize and enforce meritocracy and professional culture and behaviors ▪ A lot of communication channels to enhance transparency ▪ Leaders developing leaders in classrooms ▪ Development through job rotation and assignment

Developing a Unique Value Proposition

This research study starts with one basic question, "How can companies win the talent war and deliver extraordinary business results in regions where talent is hard to source?" As we conclude this article, we would like to recommend a roadmap (see Figure 4.1 on page 79) that companies can use to sharpen their effectiveness in winning the talent war.

Step 0: Reexamine your company talent management philosophy

This is step 0 because we believe this is a prerequisite for an effective talent management strategy. If companies do not believe that talent is critical to their business success or are not willing to invest in talent to achieve success, it is almost impossible to expect a highly engaged and committed workforce to grow with the company. The following two questions need to be candidly discussed and examined among the leadership team:

- To what extent do we REALLY believe that talent is really critical to our business success?
- What kind of relationship do we want to create with our employees? Economic exchange, under-investment, over-investment or mutual investment?

Step 1: Identify the talent that is critical to business success

Once we believe that talent is critical to business success, we then need to clearly understand what kind of talent is important in terms of both professional skills and core employee competencies. For example, Bosera Fund Management needs highly experienced and well-trained research analysts, fund managers and traders to oversee and increase the value of its fund investments. For the Portman Ritz-Carlton, they need talents who are passionate about their work and enjoy working with others. For Li-Ning, they need talents who not only have professional expertise, but also a passion for sports. In this way, they can convey more effectively the spirit of sportsmanship advocated by the company and relate to the company's sportswear designs.

Step 2: Understand the top needs and wants of this targeted talent

In order to attract, retain and engage the targeted talent to contribute to the company's success, we also need to thoroughly understand what matters to them by surveying and interviewing current and prospective employees. For example, the research analysts and fund managers whom Bosera targets deeply care about their visibility and impact within their professions. Employees of the Portman Ritz-Carlton deeply care about being respected, and having a sense of pride and achievement in doing their jobs well, in addition to earning a decent salary and having career growth opportunities. The designers and marketing talent that Li-Ning targets deeply care about the mission of building a world-class Chinese firm, developing a work culture and environment that they enjoy, and being richly rewarded for a job well done.

Step 3: Brainstorm and articulate unique value propositions that matter to both the company and targeted talent

After understanding the needs and requirements from both the employer and employee perspectives, companies should brainstorm and articulate what unique value propositions they can offer to their targeted talent that their competitors cannot offer or cannot offer so well. For Bosera Fund Management, it is to enable their talent to "pursue professional excellence in a caring and supportive organization." For the Portman Ritz-Carlton, it is to "set our ladies and gentlemen up for success." For Li-Ning, it is to provide an environment where the talent can "win globally based on sportsmanship." As companies brainstorm and develop their unique value propositions, they need to be bold and creative rather than benchmark what other companies are offering. The more distinctive and unique their values, the more powerful they are in winning the talent war beyond mere financial compensation.

Step 4: Identify key enablers and align the content and criteria with unique value propositions

Last but not least, companies need to identify key enablers that have the most immediate and direct impact on the creation of the unique value proposition. The key insight here is companies do not need to be world class in every HR practice but excel in those practices that are essential to their unique value propositions. For Bosera Fund, it is providing opportunities for professional growth through training and new product teams. For the Portman Ritz-

Carlton, it is selecting people who like to help others. For Li-Ning, it is conveying and creating a sportsmanship spirit within the company through training, communication and work style.

However, none of these enabling practices is a substitute for strong and committed leaders who consistently walk the talk regardless of whether the company is going through good or bad times. Aptly summarized by Mark DeConcinis at the Portman Ritz-Carlton, "The secret is consistency in execution."

Conclusion

While this article describes how Best Employers win the talent war in China, we believe the underlying talent management philosophy and strategy should be highly relevant to other Asian economies such as India, Indonesia and Thailand that are facing talent shortage as their economies take off.

In this concluding remark, we would also like to highlight the implications of unique value proposition to Western multinational firms and Asian local firms. As an economy develops, we observe that the comparative advantages of Western multinational firms and Asian local firms in competing for talent evolve over time. In the early stage of any economic development like the 1960s in Hong Kong, 1970s in Taiwan or 1980s in the People's Republic of China, we observe that Western multinational firms can always out-compete local firms by offering stronger company brand, superior training and development opportunities, and more attractive compensation packages. However, as economies continue to evolve, some national champions (e.g., Alibaba.com, Lenovo, Tencent in China or Tata, Wipro, Infosys in India) rapidly emerge and can gain substantial leverage in attracting, retaining and engaging high-caliber talent by offering faster career development opportunities, generous stock options and greater empowerment to make quick decisions rather than waiting for approval from headquarters. At this stage, the talent war becomes very fierce as witnessed in the current stage of economic development in China. As we observe in the seven Best Employers (four of them are local Chinese firms and three are Western multinational firms) in the study, Asian and Western firms can win in their own ways. The key to success is to identify some unique values or strengths that they can offer to the targeted talent. For Western multinational firms, the opportunity to develop internationally oriented careers, a strong global company brand, formalized learning and development opportunities, and professional management systems and cultures are common selling points.

For local Asian firms, the opportunity to grow fast through stretched targets, generous stock option and wealth creation through IPO opportunity, no glass ceiling, appeal to patriotic pride, informal and entrepreneurial work culture, are value propositions that they can draw upon. To be different by capitalizing the relative strengths of their firms and to make such value propositions real through leadership commitment are ultimate differentiators in winning the talent war.

FIGURE 4-1. ROADMAP IN DEVELOPING AND DESIGNING UNIQUE VALUE PROPOSITIONS FOR TALENT MANAGEMENT

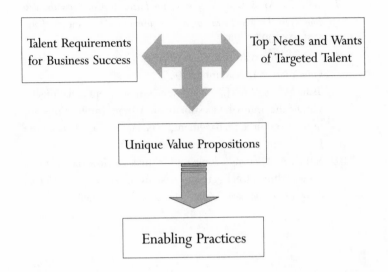

Endnotes

1. These Best Employers are elected by the three most credible organizations in China: Hewitt Associates/*Wall Street Journal*, Wyatt/*Fortune China*, and China Central Television (CCTV).

2. United Nations Conference on Trade and Development, "World Investment Report 2008, China Foreign Direct Investment (FDI) overview," www.unctad.org, 2008.

3. Ministry of Commerce of the People's Republic of China, "MOC: Major Achievements in Economic and Trade Field of Open Door Policy in the Past 30 Years," www.gov.cn, 2008.

4. Ministry of Commerce of the People's Republic of China, "FDI in China, recall 2008, forecast 2009," *China Investment Guidance*, 2009.

5. Yang, Y., "Multinational firms in China in the last two decades," *Foreign Investment in China*, No. 12, Research Institute of Department of Commerce, 2005.

6. Farrell, D. & Grant, A., "China's Looming Talent Shortage," *McKinsey Quarterly*, November 2005.

7. Bennett, M. & Bell, A., *Leadership Talent in Asia: How the Best Employers Deliver Extraordinary Performance* (Singapore: John Wiley), 2004.

8. Watson Wyatt/*Fortune China*, "Work China Survey," *Fortune China*, No. 84, November 2005.

9. Tsui, A. & Wu, J., "The new employment relationship versus the mutual investment approach: Implications for human resource management," *Human Resource Management Journal,* Vol. 44, No. 2, (Summer 2005).

10. Yeung, A., "Setting people up for success: How the Portman Ritz-Carlton Hotel gets the best from its people," *Human Resource Management Journal*, 45, No. 2 (Summer 2006).

CHAPTER 5

Global Leadership Practices Among Large Multinational Companies
How Asia Compares

Patrick M. Wright

Executive Summary

As Asian economies increasingly lead the world in growth, companies in Asia need to evolve their leadership development practices. This paper presents some results from a study examining the global leadership development practices used by large multinational companies, and explores the extent to which a variety of practices are used as well as the extent to which respondents believed they were global best practices. The results demonstrate that, for most practices, Asian operations largely resemble that of the rest of the world (with Korean operations tending to be the exception).

In spite of the current global economic recession, growth in Asia continues. This growth has moved from simply being a function of low-cost manufacturing operations towards high skilled, high technology, discovery and development work. While the pace of growth has slowed during the recession, companies doing business in Asia still face tremendous difficulties in attracting and retaining talent.

In particular, one form of talent that Asian companies demand is leadership talent. Many Asian countries are quite adept at building technical talent through their educational systems, but find that the demand for leadership still exceeds its supply. Thus, one key to future success in Asia will be a company's ability to leverage its HR practices to build a pool of effective leaders. However, what practices effectively do so, and to what extent are these practices being leveraged in Asia? This chapter reports the results of a large-scale survey of global HR practices among large multinational companies. While only a few of these companies are headquartered in Asia, the survey gathered data from the country heads of HR in each of 30 different countries to examine the extent to which those leadership development practices are being used and the extent to which the respondents believed that they were effective best practices.

Study Methodology

This study was conducted in three phases. In the first phase, a doctoral student researcher conducted an extensive literature review aimed at identifying all of the HR practices that have been identified in the academic literature as "effective best practices." These practices were defined as practices that researchers have either posited or empirically demonstrated to be linked to positive employee and organizational outcomes.

Second, the Global Human Resource Research Consortium (GHRRC) team conducted a series of case studies aimed at identifying those "best practices" that companies suggested they had used to manage their workforce as a source of competitive advantage. Eighteen case companies were selected based on their superior business performance and reputation as an employer as defined through 2004 *Fortune* listings and equivalent rankings.

During 2004–05, interviews were held with 295 people across 20 countries (Belgium, Brazil, China, Dubai, France, Germany, Hong Kong, India, Italy, Japan, Korea, Malaysia, Netherlands, Norway, Singapore, Spain, Sweden, Switzerland, UK, USA) (see Table 5.1). On average, approximately 15 to 20 interviews per company were conducted. A multiple-respondent approach was adopted, including interviews with 174 HR professionals and 121 non-HR staff (senior executives, line managers and employee representatives). The research was also multilevel: 122 of the interviews were carried out at corporate headquarters, 103 at either country or divisional head office level, and 70 at unit level within a specific business division.

The interviews were semistructured, based on a schedule designed and piloted by the academic partners, covering questions about the business context, HRM practices and the HR function. Across the first two phases of the study we identified the population of best practices that have emerged from academic research and successful global organizations.

The final phase of the study consisted of a quantitative survey assessing the extent to which the best HR practices are used in a variety of countries across a sample of large multinational companies. The results of this survey are reported here.

Sample

The Survey Research Institute (SRI) at Cornell University was contracted to host and administer the survey over the Web. An initial email went out to companies requesting contact information for top HR leaders in a list of 36 countries. The list was generated in a two-step process. First, we gathered the rankings of countries based on their Gross Domestic Product (GDP) as identified through the World Bank. Using this list, we then sought to identify a sample of the higher GDP (assuming that they were more likely to have MNC presence) countries within the regions of North America, Western Europe, Central/Eastern Europe, Latin America, Asia, Southeast Asia, Central Asia and Africa. It is important to note that the list was generated for ensuring geographical dispersion, but it was not based on any assumptions regarding similarity of HR orientations. This list is provided in Table 5.1.

TABLE 5-1. COUNTRIES STUDIED FOR LEADERSHIP PRACTICES

North America	Latin America
United States	Brazil
Canada	Argentina
Mexico	Venezuela

Western Europe	Asia
Germany	Japan
United Kingdom	Korea
France	China
Italy	
Spain	Southeast Asia
Netherlands	Australia
Switzerland	Indonesia
Sweden	Thailand
Greece	Malaysia

Central/Eastern Europe
Russian Federation
Poland
Czech Republic
Slovakia
Hungary

Southeast Asia (cont'd)
Singapore
Vietnam

Central Asia
India
Israel
Turkey
United Arab Emirates

Africa
South Africa
Nigeria
Egypt

We invited a set of approximately 50 multinational companies to participate in the global survey. Twenty of them agreed to do so. This sample of 20 companies consisted of 14 having headquarters located in the United States, four in Europe and two in Asia. Thus, in interpreting the results of this study, one must note that, while the sample of respondents is not overly biased towards U.S.-based respondents, the respondents are, overall, disproportionately employed by U.S.-based firms. These companies are listed in Table 5.2.

TABLE 5-2. MULTINATIONAL COMPANIES PARTICIPATING IN THE SURVEY

Participating Organizations

ABB	Citigroup	EMC	Firstdata
Gap	General Electric	General Mills	GlaxoSmithKline
IBM	IKEA	Lucent	MassMutual
Nissan	Proctor & Gamble	Rolls-Royce	SK
TNT	Underwriter Labs	Wachovia	Xerox

Of those wishing to participate, we sent an Excel file with the 36 countries listed and asked them to provide the contact information for the most senior HR office in each of the countries in which they had a significant presence. Thus, some companies provided only ten contacts because they had presence in only ten of the 26 countries. The number of respondents per subregion ranged from nine to 39 and averaged 20 respondents.

Once we received the contact information, we sent the potential respondents an email inviting them to participate in the study. In the body of the message was a link to the online survey. We sent out two rounds of reminders to potential respondents who had not responded approximately three weeks apart. Of the total respondents, 239 fell into regional categories while 236 fell into subregions. This difference stems from the fact that three respondents self reported that they were responsible for a particular region (Americas, Asia Pacific or EMEA) rather than a specific country. Thus, in reports of subregion (to be discussed later) level data, the sample is based on the 236 respondents who specified their country. See Table 5.3.

TABLE 5-3. NUMBER OF PARTICIPANTS BY REGION

Region	Total Participants
Americas	59
AP (Asia Pacific)	67
EMEA (Europe, Middle East & Africa)	113
Total:	**239**
Overall Number of Participants: 263	

(Note: Some respondents could not be assigned to a specific subregion or region.)

Once the data was gathered, for the purposes of analyses, we sought to categorize the countries into subregions. While we had originally hoped to conduct all our analyses at the country level, for a number of countries, we had three or fewer respondents. To report such data would (a) limit the extent to which we could ensure confidentiality of respondents and (b) provide relatively unstable or idiosyncratic measurement of the focal practices. Thus, we grouped the countries using the criterion that the countries should have been shown by previous research to be similar to each other and distinct from their neighbors in the sets or configurations of HR practices. Table 5.4 displays the number of respondents in each of the 12 subregions. Note that all but two of the 12 subregions have greater than ten respondents. It should also be noted that each country had a maximum of one respondent per country, but when combined into subregions, there might be more than one respondent per company (e.g., if a company had respondents from Singapore, Vietnam and Malaysia, they might have three respondents within the Southeast Asia subregion).

TABLE 5-4. NUMBER OF PARTICIPANTS BY SUBREGION

Americas	Latin America	20
	North America	39
	Total:	**59**
AP (Asia Pacific)	China Affiliated	12
	Japan	14
	Korea	13
	Southeast Asia	27
	Total:	**66**
EMEA (Europe, Middle East, and Africa)	British Isles	30
	Central and Eastern Europe	17
	Middle East and Africa	9
	Northern Europe	9
	Rhineland	27
	Southern Europe	19
	Total:	**111**

Measures

The survey itself was generated through the following process. First, a set of graduate students conducted an exhaustive review of the academic literature on HR practices and performance, attempting to identify a list of practices that have been used as measures of "best" HR practices (i.e., those that should be associated with higher firm performance). Second, while conducting the case studies described previously, we sought to identify practices that the company interviewees thought constituted the best HR practices that might not have been identified in the academic literature. The potential pool of practices was then reviewed by all members of the research team (four professors and three graduate students) to identify the relevant practices and ensure that the wording would be understandable across the global sample. These practices were organized into six major areas: Staffing (10 practices), Training and Development (11 practices), Appraisal (14 practices), Rewards (11 practices), Employee Relations (10 practices), and Leadership and Succession (8 practices). It is important to note that the team sought to identify practices that might be considered the best practices in a particular country or culture (e.g., seniority-based promotions or rewards) but they might not be considered best practices using a Western management view. This chapter will focus only on the Leadership and Succession practices.

HR Practices

The first section of the survey sought to examine the set of HR best practices within respondents' countries along two dimensions. First, respondents were asked to indicate "To what extent do you use the following practice?" for each of the HR practices listed. This measure captures the usage of practices and it answers the question "Are different HR practices used differentially across geographies?" However, unlike other surveys of HR practices that only focus on usage, we sought to indicate perceptions regarding the effectiveness of the practices. For instance, one could identify situations where a practice is used because of institutional requirements, yet not perceived to be an effective practice. Conversely, one could think of situations where certain practices which are thought to be quite effective have not been implemented for either institutional or cultural reasons. Thus, for each practice, the respondents were also asked to answer "To what extent do you find this practice effective for managing people?" This dimension captures the perception of whether or not a practice should be considered a best practice and can answer the question "Is the effectiveness of HR practices perceived differentially across geographies?" It is important to note that respondents were asked to rate the effectiveness of the practice even if they did not use it.

In addition, assessing both dimensions simultaneously allows us to identify practices where there are gaps between use and effectiveness. While the ordinal nature of the data does not allow exact comparisons along these two dimensions because respondents were answering the questions in tandem, it is highly likely that negative gaps (e.g., higher effectiveness ratings than use ratings) indicate that respondents believe that the practice could be effective if used more, and positive gaps (higher use than effective-ness) indicate that respondents believe that the practices are not as effective and should be used less.

Finally, within this section, respondents then looked across the major practice areas and made overall assessments along the following three dimensions: Alignment,

Commitment and Flexibility. Alignment focuses on the extent to which the practices are aligned with the firm's key strategies and goals. Commitment represents the extent to which managers are committed to the practices. Flexibility indicates the extent to which the practices are flexible for meeting the shifting demands of the business.

Thus, the rest of this chapter will focus on reporting the results of the Leadership and Succession practices of:

1. A scheme to develop potential leaders
2. A scheme to identify potential leaders
3. A defined set of leadership competencies
4. Leadership behaviors linked to business performance
5. A high percentage of elite hires from outside the firm
6. Potential leaders are rotated through functions
7. Formal succession processes in place
8. Potential leaders are given challenging assignments

In addition, one of the items from the Training and Development section focused specifically on the extent to which firms had made formal investments in Leadership Development, so we begin with discussing the results from that question, and then focus on the results from the more specific Leadership Development practices.

Formal Investments in Leadership Development

Global responses indicated the extent to which their company had made formal investments in leadership development within their specific country of responsibility and these results can be observed in Figure 5.1. Overall, the results indicated a mean use response of 3.77 and a mean effectiveness response of 4.10, indicating that most respondents seemed to have made formal investments in leadership development but they recognized that they could do better here. The greatest usage of leadership development was reported in the British Isles, and the greatest gap between use and effectiveness was observed in the Middle East and Africa which reported both the lowest use and highest belief in the practice's effectiveness as a best practice.

In particular, the Asian subregions (China Affiliated, Japan, Korea and Southeast Asia) all fell around the average in both use and effectiveness, and thus look pretty much like the rest of the developed world.

FIGURE 5-1. FORMAL INVESTMENTS IN LEADERSHIP DEVELOPMENT

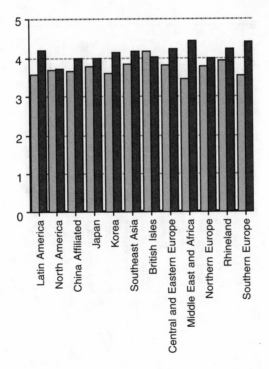

Formal Scheme to Develop Potential Leaders

Effective leadership development cannot be haphazard. It must consist of a systematic set of tools and processes aimed at developing high potential leaders. Thus, respondents were asked to indicate the extent to which their company in their country had developed a formal system or scheme for developing potential leaders, as well as the extent to which they believe such a practice would be effective. These results are shown in Figure 5.2.

The overall mean for the use was 3.53 and the overall mean for effectiveness perceptions was 4.09, indicating that

FIGURE 5-2. A FORMAL SCHEME TO DEVELOP POTENTIAL LEADERS

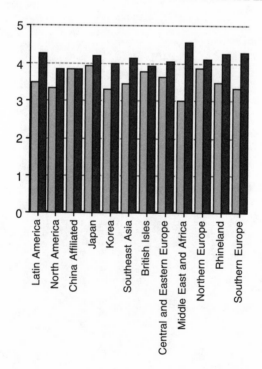

most companies have some formal scheme, and that this is believed to be an effective best practice. Interestingly, these results indicate high variability in use within Asia. For instance, Japanese respondents reported the highest use of the development scheme and Korea was among the lowest across all the subregions. On the other hand, the belief that such a practice is an effective best practice was equally shared across all the Asian subregions as well as across all the global subregions.

Formal Scheme to Identify Potential Leaders

Identifying high potential leaders cannot be done through random assignment. It should be done through a formal set of systems, tools and processes aimed at differentiating with regard to leadership potential. Thus, the next practice examined was with regard to a formal system or scheme to identify potential leaders. Such a practice aims at having systematic processes for picking out those who have high potential as leaders. These results are displayed in Figure 5.3.

Almost identical to the previous practice, the overall mean use response was 3.49 and the overall effectiveness response was 4.06. However, as can be seen in Figure 5.3, there seems to be more variability in the use and effectiveness responses. Again, Japan was among the highest in use and Korea among the lowest in use. China and Southeast Asia were around the average for the rest of the globe. On the other hand, Japan and Southeast Asia were among the highest in the belief that this is an effective best practice, and Korea, while still reasonably high, was among the lowest in this belief.

FIGURE 5-3. A FORMAL SCHEME TO IDENTIFY POTENTIAL LEADERS

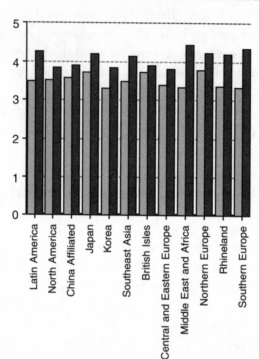

Defined Leadership Competencies

A recent trend in leadership development has been towards developing formal leadership competency models. Such models define somewhere between 10 and 25 general competencies that leaders must have, and many of these models more specifically define the behaviors associated with each competency. The results with regard to this general item are displayed in Figure 5.4.

Overall, this leadership practice had the highest use of any at 3.9, and a high (4.09) score on effectiveness. This seems to indicate that this practice is central to leadership

FIGURE 5-4. THE COMPANY HAS DEFINED LEADERSHIP COMPETENCIES

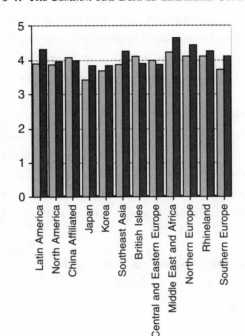

development across the globe. Interestingly, China was among the highest in reported use when compared to the other subregions, and Japan was the lowest, again indicating variability within the Asian context. However, all of the Asian subregions (China, Japan, Korea and Southeast Asia) reported the belief that competency models are an effective best practice, very similar to the rest of the globe.

Leadership Behaviors Linked to Business Performance

One question regarding leadership development concerns the extent to which companies are able to link leader behavior to business performance. This can be done conceptually by attempting to identify a set of behaviors where a link can be articulated to business performance, or empirically demonstrating that certain behaviors are statistically correlated with performance. The results to this practice can be seen in Figure 5.5.

The results indicate that this is a practice that is predominantly used by firms (3.49) and is seen as reasonably effective (4.06). Southeast Asia was the subregion that reported the highest use of this practice across the entire sample, and Japan was among the lowest. In addition, Southeast Asia was among the highest in the belief in the practice's effectiveness.

FIGURE 5-5. LEADERSHIP BEHAVIORS ARE LINKED TO BUSINESS PERFORMANCE

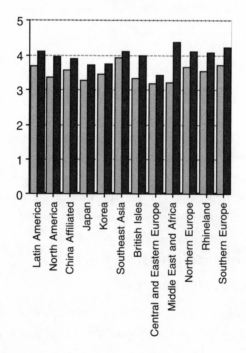

Elite Hires from Outside

As leadership talent becomes more important in a market without adequate supply, many firms resort to hiring leaders from outside. This may be driven by short-term necessity when existing development programs are not fully functioning, or it may be a long-term strategy to not having to invest as much in internal development. These results are displayed in Figure 5.6.

Overall, this was the second-lowest rated leadership practice in terms of use (2.87) and the lowest rated practice regarding the belief in its effectiveness (3.17). This indicates that for the most part, firms prefer not to have to resort to this as a means of gaining leadership talent, but that it is one

FIGURE 5-6. HIGH PROPORTION OF ELITE HIRES FROM OUTSIDE THE ORGANIZATION

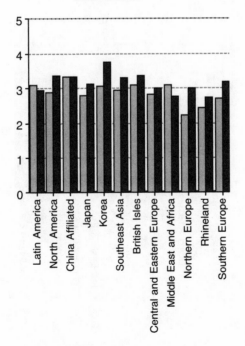

practice they must keep in their arsenal. Interestingly, Korea reported the highest effectiveness of this practice across the globe. In addition, in the war for talent within, Asia, China, Korea and Southeast Asia were among the highest in the use of elite hires from outside the firm.

Rotating Leaders Through Various Functions

Many believe that to be an effective leader at the top of the organization requires a broader and more general view of the firm, and that this is best accomplished through a series of job assignments outside of a potential leader's area of functional expertise. The results regarding this practice can be seen in Figure 5.7.

FIGURE 5-7. POTENTIAL LEADERS ARE ROTATED THROUGH FUNCTIONS

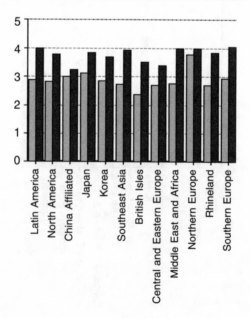

Overall, this practice had the lowest use rating (2.83) of all the practices studied. With a rating of 3.76 regarding the belief in its effectiveness as a best practice, this leadership item had the highest gap between use and effectiveness.

All four of the Asian subregions exhibited means of around 3 on use, which although rather low, was on the higher side across the globe. In addition, China Affiliated respondents reported the absolute lowest belief in the practice's effectiveness at just over 3 while the rest of Asia (and indeed, much of the rest of the globe) reported effectiveness ratings closer to 4 on the 5-point scale.

Succession Planning/Replacement Charts

Given the short tenure of CEOs today and the increasing mobility of talent, many firms have increasingly emphasized the importance of going through a formal succession planning process. When done in a thorough manner, such a process results in specific replacement charts such that for every senior leader, there is a list of potential replacements should that leader depart suddenly.

This practice received an overall use rating of 3.47 and an overall effectiveness rating of 3.89, indicating that it is a reasonably popular practice that respondents believe provides some value. Interestingly, this practice had a high degree of variability in responses, both across the globe and within Asia. For instance, Middle East and Africa's respondents were by far the lowest in use (approximately 2.5) and among the lowest in effectiveness (around 3), while Japan had the highest use (3.5) and effectiveness (4.1). In addition, within Asia, Korea stood out with low use (under 3) and effectiveness ratings (3). See Figure 5.8.

FIGURE 5-8. FORMAL SUCCESSION PLANNING WITH REPLACEMENT CHARTS

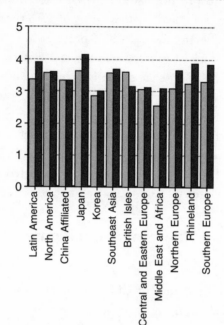

Leaders Given Challenging Assignments

Part of the development of effective leaders often revolves around putting them in challenging assignments. Such assignments can help them hone their leadership skills and make visible to decision-makers a leader's specific strengths and weaknesses. The results regarding this practice are displayed in Figure 5.9.

Overall, this practice received the highest rating regarding the belief that it constitutes an effective best practice (4.14), but was only average in regard to its use (3.50). This indicates another practice that seems to have a rather large gap between its use and effectiveness.

Within Asia, China Affiliated, Japan and Southeast Asia all reported a high level of belief in the effectiveness of

FIGURE 5-9. POTENTIAL LEADERS ARE GIVEN CHALLENGING ASSIGNMENTS

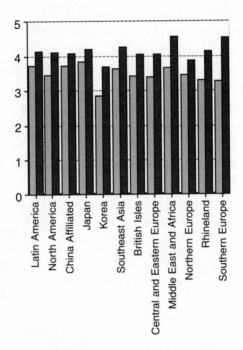

using challenging assignments (all over 4) and a relatively (compared to other subregions) high level of use. Korea was clearly an outlier here, with the lowest use by far (under 3) and the lowest belief in its effectiveness.

Strategic Alignment, Managerial Commitment and Flexibility

Our literature search revealed that there are three additional dimensions to HR practices that seem necessary for the practices to have maximal effectiveness: alignment with strategy, commitment of managers and flexibility. Thus, after responding to the specific practices, we asked respondents to rate the general areas of HR practice with regard to each of these dimensions.

One criticism of HR practice in general has been that some HR functions focus on developing best practices in terms of their technical superiority, but fail to develop practices that are aligned with the strategic needs of the business. Regarding alignment of the leadership development practices with business strategy, the results in Figure 5.10 showed that across the globe, firms seem to still have some room for improvement. Only in the region of Northern Europe was the rating above 4. Within Asia, Japan respondents reported the highest alignment and Korean respondents reported the lowest.

FIGURE 5-10. ALIGNMENT OF LEADERSHIP PRACTICES WITH BUSINESS STRATEGY

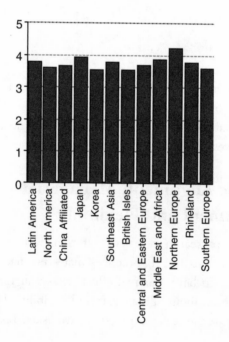

No matter how well designed a practice is, most practices are actually delivered by line managers. Thus, in addition to the necessity of alignment, if managers are not committed to the practices, they can never reach their potential effectiveness. See Figure 5.11.

Interestingly, respondents across the globe reported a relatively low level of managerial commitment to leadership practices (between 3.1 and 3.9). Again, Northern Europe reported the highest level of commitment. Within Asia, respondents from Japan reported the highest level of commitment, and the other three subregions were quite close to one another in the 3.4 to 3.5 range.

FIGURE 5-11. MANAGERS' COMMITMENT TO LEADERSHIP PRACTICES

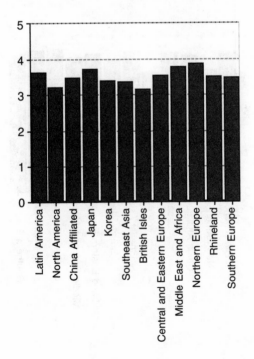

Finally, in the fast-changing competitive environment most firms face today, HR practices need to be flexible and adaptable. Sadly, leadership practices seem to be lacking in this regard, as shown in the results in Figure 5.12. Across the globe, respondents reported flexibility ratings no higher than 3.6 on a 5-point scale, far below the other two dimensions of strategy alignment and managerial commitment. With regard to Asia, specifically, Korea had the lowest ratings (3.0, and lowest across the global sample) with the other three Asia subregions being relatively equal to one another and among the highest across the globe.

FIGURE 5-12. FLEXIBILITY OF LEADERSHIP PRACTICES

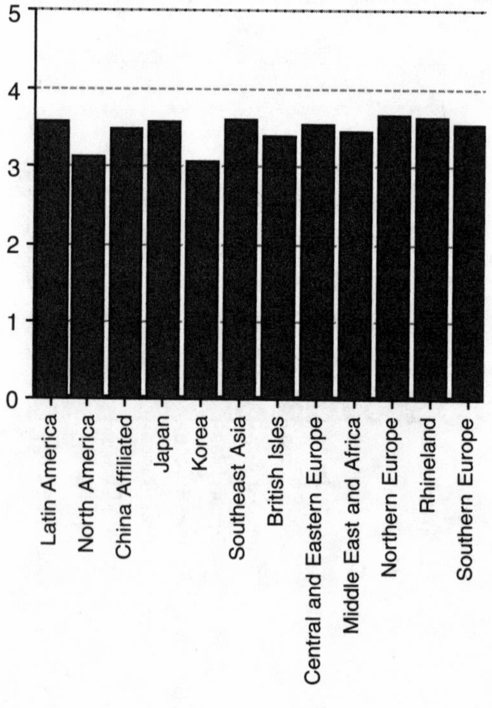

Caveats and Limitations

Before discussing the conclusions, one must recognize the limitations of this data. First, the sample size of 20 companies does not provide a large representative sample of the population of multinational companies. Thus, the sample size alone limits how firmly one should draw conclusions regarding the global leadership practices being used.

Second, the makeup of the sample companies was heavily weighted towards U.S.- and UK-based companies with relatively fewer Europe- and Asia-based companies. Thus, if one believes that a large component of leadership development practices is determined from company headquarters, these results may disproportionately reflect how U.S.- and UK-based companies seek to develop leaders within their Asian operations. This implies that perhaps larger differences might be observed between the Asian leadership development practices and the rest of the world if Asia-based companies comprised a greater percentage of the sample. Hence, with these limitations in mind, I suggest the following conclusions.

Summary and Conclusions

Multinational companies increasingly face challenges in managing a global workforce. HR practices (including leadership practices) often need to be tailored to, or at least adapted to, the local regulatory and cultural environment. This study examined how the same set of multinational companies tends to differentially implement leadership practices across their global operations.

In general, it seems that a global convergence of what constitutes best practices seems to be emerging, at least among multinational companies. What is striking in looking across all of the leadership practices is how small the differences are, far smaller than one would expect given the arguments about different leadership styles and cultural constraints that exist across countries. In particular, while there were greater differences in the use of practices, there is far greater convergence with regard to the belief in the effectiveness of those practices.

Within Asia, a few trends could be observed. First, it appears that Japan seems to be the most advanced in terms of formal practices aimed at developing leaders, but not as far along in the trend towards using competencies as the basis around which the practices are aimed. Korean operations, on the other hand, reflect the exact opposite trend. Operations in this country seem to have moved far along in the development of competencies for leaders, but seem to be less advanced in the implementation of formal practices aimed at developing those competencies.

Finally, China Affiliated and Southeast Asian operations reflect an approach to leadership development appropriate within the context of an intense war for talent. On most of the formal practices, operations within these areas have been implemented at a relatively high level. On the other hand, job rotations seem to be used significantly less. In an environment where turnover is high, companies need as much stability as possible where leadership is concerned, and thus it is not unexpected that job rotations (which systematically build turnover into assignments in addition to the turnover that is going on as individuals leave the firm) would not seem to be as useful for maintaining stability.

Finally, operations in Asia generally do not differ substantially from operations across the rest of the globe. In addition, the differences that do emerge are differences within

Asia, reinforcing the idea that to talk about "HR in Asia" is a rather futile effort. In some practices, Japan emerged at the top and Korea at the bottom, while on other practices, Korea was at the top and Japan was at the bottom. This illustrates the need to further explore the differences across Asia, which are, seemingly, as large as the differences across the globe.

CHAPTER 6

Waging and Winning the War for Talent in Asia

J. Stewart Black

Take 20 seconds and answer the quiz below:

1.	Does the quality of talent make a difference to the bottom-line results in your business?	Yes	No
2.	Do you believe people are your most important assets?	Yes	No
3.	Does your company seek to be the employer of choice in your industry?	Yes	No
4.	Is it harder these days to find, attract, keep, and keep engaged the best talent?	Yes	No
5.	Do you have a clear strategy for being the employer of choice and winning the war for talent?	Yes	No
6.	Do you have good metrics for calibrating how you are doing as an employer of choice?	Yes	No
7.	Do you hold managers and executives accountable for their success and failure in waging and winning the war for talent?	Yes	No

If you are like 98 percent of the over 5,000 executives across more than 500 companies who hail from over 100 countries that I have surveyed, you answered "yes" to questions 1 to 4 and answered "no" to questions 5 to 7. This is disturbing because if you believe that differentiated human capital is critical to differentiated business performance but do not have clear strategies, metrics and accountabilities, then you are headed for trouble, especially if you are going forward in Asia.

I say this because the war for talent in Asia is only going to heat up. In fact, despite the economic downturn in 2008 and 2009, my research suggests that the war for talent in Asia will likely last another 20 years! Companies that recognize this and leaders who proactively measure, monitor and enhance their employee value proposition will be the ones who will win the war for talent and the battles for competitive position.

Drivers of the War for Talent

How can I say that the war for talent in Asia is only going to heat up and will last another 20 years? It is because there are four major changes that have made employees a firm's most important asset and have shifted the balance of power from the employer to the employee. Below I discuss each of these four shifts and integrate their implication at the end.

Shift in Competitive Advantage

Historically, much of an organization's competitive advantage rested in its tangible assets—its property, equipment, tools and the proprietary aspects of its products. People were more like interchangeable gears that simply kept the machine moving. As we have moved increasingly into a service- and knowledge-based economy, intangibles such as service, solutions, culture, brand and leadership are becoming the basis upon which companies gain competitive advantage. Most of these intangible sources of advantage are either people or are largely driven by people. For example, many companies have cultures that they believe give them advantages in customer service and cross-unit collaboration that allows them to deliver integrated solutions. Take people out of the culture and what do you have left? Not much. This shift in competitive advantage from tangibles to intangibles have unwittingly shifted the power in the employment relationship from leaning heavily in the favor of the employer to leaning more towards the employee and raised the consequences (positive and negative) of winning the war for the best people.

Shift in Information Symmetry

In the past, there was significant information asymmetry regarding the supply and demand for talent as well as the compensation paid. In other words, employers were the ones that really knew if the demand for a certain type of employee was going up or down, whether the supply was high or low, and what was happening to the wages relative to those employees. This is in part because if an organization wanted to know this information about a certain category of employees, say Java language programrs, the organization could hire Mercer or whomever to do a market study for them. The company could then amortize the cost of the US$200,000 market study across the 1,000 Java pro-grammers it had. Thus, the per-employee cost to the company would be US$200. In contrast, if a single Java programr wanted to know this same information—if the demand for Java programrs was going up or down, whether the supply was high or low, and what was happening to the wages for Java programrs—the lone employee would have to pay Mercer the US$200,000 for the market study and amortize it across one person! As a consequence in the past, employers generally knew this type of information and employees did not.

While the Internet did not change everything, it did tear this information asymmetry apart. Now, employees can go for free onto a site like Monster.com and in 10 minutes they can know quite a bit about the supply, demand and wages in the market for their skills. This shift in information symmetry from employers enjoying a significant asymmetric advantage to employees knowing as much (or maybe even more) than employers has unwittingly shifted the power in the employment relationship from leaning heavily in the favor of the employer to leaning more towards the employee. This, like the first shift, has raised the consequences (positive and negative) of winning the war for the best people.

Shift in Company-Specific Benefits

As recently as 1985, over 70 percent of non-government organizations had defined retirement benefit programs and only 30 percent had defined contribution programs. Today, these numbers are completely reversed. While these are undisputed facts, the question is what impact do they have on the war for talent? To understand the answer, we have to first remind ourselves of the nature of the two different types of retirement schemes. In the case of defined benefit programs, the financial payment one would receive after retirement was "defined" or predetermined. These definitions varied but most were back-end weighted meaning that the value of the defined benefit came primarily from some percentage of the last few years of an employee's compensation. For example, the defined retirement benefit might be 65 percent of the average annual salary for the last five years of employment. This created a natural economic incentive to stay with a company. With defined contribution plans, only the contribution the employer pays is defined—not what the employee gets in the end. For example, the contribution might be 7 percent of your current monthly salary. Typically, the defined contribution stays the same even as an employee's tenure in the company increases. The financial impact of this change was that retirement related obligations were much more predictable and therefore their impact on earnings was also more predictable (and this is why most CFOs argued for the switch). The employment impact was that these defined contribution plans were more portable than defined benefit plans and thus lowered an employee's switching costs in moving from one employer to another. Just as when the switching cost for customers are lower, the intensity of the competition for customers goes up, so too has been the impact on the war for talent. In summary, the shift from defined benefit to defined contribution plans has lowered employee switching costs and thereby increased their leverage in the employment relationship.

Shift in Supply and Demand

The fourth and arguably the most important shift affecting the war for talent has been a significant shift in the balance between supply and demand, especially in Asia. For example, McKinsey in 2005[1] conducted a study in which they estimated that the supply of managers in China who could work effectively in a multinational company was about 5,000 but the demand was 75,000. Whether these numbers are exactly right or not, if they are directionally correct, then we should see wages rising to offset the imbalance between supply and demand. This is exactly what we have seen. Wages in China for managers have risen at about 10 to 20 percent per year over the last decade. This same imbalance can be seen in other countries in Asia such as Vietnam and India. This is not because these countries do not have enough people. Rather, the supply-demand imbalance comes from the lack of people with the requisite experience. Most of this lack of quality supply simply comes from a dearth of educational and work opportunities in sufficient quantity and quality to produce the numbers and types of people in demand today.

Let us first take a quick look at education and its role in the supply-demand imbalance. While the percentage of people attending university in all these countries is going up, the participation rate is less than half what one would find in developed countries and is not keeping up with demand. For example, in Vietnam, demand for workers with vocational training in 2010 is expected to be 500,000 while supply is expected to grow to only 55,000. Furthermore, in most of the countries in Asia, if one looks at the investment rate in the quality of facilities and instructors, one notices it is not keeping pace with either the increase in the number of students or the employment demands. For example, in Vietnam, the student-faculty ratio at universities went from 4.7-to-1 in 1986 to 15.3-to-1 by 2004.

While improvements in the quantity of education available and the quality provided can and will likely increase, these are changes that in vast countries like China, India and Vietnam will take decades to fully implement. In the meantime, for virtually all industries and companies, Asia remains the one bright spot of potential growth and therefore ever growing demand for talent. This shift in growing demand and trailing supply has unwittingly shifted the power in the employment relationship from leaning heavily in the favor of the employer to leaning more towards the employee, especially those in the service and knowledge areas. This, like the three other shifts, has raised the consequences (positive and negative) of winning the war for the best people.

Implications

As far as I can determine, none of the four shifts I have described seems temporary—none of these genies seems like they can be put back in the bottle. As a consequence, the war for talent, especially in areas such as high service intensity such as education, consultancy, financial services, technology and pharmaceuticals, is likely to get more intense before it gets less intense. The consequences for waging and winning these battles, as well as for losing, are likely only to grow.

The good news is that, based on my research, companies that have a superior Employee Value Proposition (EVP) can have levels of talent retention that are twice as good as firms with unsystematic, nonstrategic and therefore poorer EVPs. My research also suggests that there are multiple configurations for a superior EVP. In other words, it is not the case that you must pay more than the market rate to win the war for talent. But it is the case that if one of the elements of the EVP, compensation for example, is not superior, then some other elements must be superior for the overall EVP to be superior and deliver the desired benefits. The strategic configuration of the EVP in which some, but not necessarily all, elements are superior in order to achieve an overall attractive and effective EVP requires strategic and deliberate discussion, decisions and actions. Superior EVPs do not just happen by accident.

Creating a Superior Employee Value Proposition

Even though a large and growing number of executives recognize that waging and winning the war for talent is critical for their business success, they complain about the "woolly" or "fuzzy" nature of the Employee Value Proposition that is usually presented and of the approaches offered for attracting and retaining the best and brightest. "Employer of choice" is an oft-quoted phrase but translating it into concrete assessments and actions has remained a challenge in the minds of most business executives. In the remainder of this chapter, I outline a technique and tool that I have developed and tested on real companies that take this critical issue from the abstract to the actionable.

Value Proposition—The Basics

As with customers, if you want to attract and retain the best and brightest talent, you have to offer a superior value proposition. Fundamentally, employees have to believe that working for you is more attractive than their best, realistic alternative. This is because employees, like customers, have choices and are free to change employers, and the value proposition from the employer to the employee (i.e., the EVP) has to be sufficiently attractive that prospective employees choose you over competitors and stay loyal to you despite alternatives. This is why the tool I present is in actuality borrowed from marketing and adapted to the challenge of attracting and retaining talent.

The best way to explain how to assess and then create a compelling Employee Value Proposition is to first describe the technique and tool as it has been used in marketing to attract and retain customers and then relate it back to its application with employees. Several years ago, marketers and academics were searching for a means of measuring the value proposition to a customer so that companies could better predict a product's ability to attract and retain customers. There was particular interest in figuring out the components of an attractive value proposition in terms of retaining customers because retained customers are some of the most profitable. In this search, they found that a simple matrix composed of two dimensions—price and offering—accounted for roughly 20 percent of the factors that explained 80 percent of the results.

The first part of the tool focuses on price. All customers pay a price for a product or service. In all but the rarest of situations, customers face an array of prices for similar products and services. As a consequence, an individual firm can examine the price they charge to customers relative to the average price for a comparison group of competitors. Simplified, the price a particular company charges for a particular product is either at a discount, on par or at a premium relative to the comparison average. For example, in the area of cars, Mercedes charges a price premium, while Kia charges a price discount.

The second part of the tool looks at the product or service offering—essentially the features of the product or service. For example, in the case of a car, the offering might involve features such as styling, fuel economy, performance and handling. Using this tool, the value of a specific product or service to the customer is determined by looking at the *intersection* of the price paid and the features offered.

This intersection provides a graphical illustration of what customers get relative to what they pay. However, because customers have alternatives, this intersection is plotted in the context of a comparison average.

The diagonal line in the matrix below (Figure 6.1) represents theoretical equal value. It is called the equal value line because every intersection that ends up on the line represents an increment in features that is matched by a proportional increment in price. Consequently, superior values are above the line, while inferior ones are below the line.

FIGURE 6-1. VALUE PROPOSITION

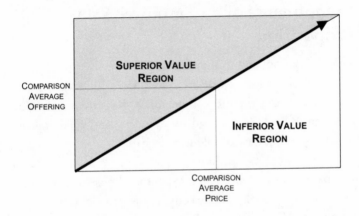

For example, Singapore Airlines charges a slight premium price for long-haul travel compared to other major airlines. However, there are objective ratings that clearly show that its onboard service, food, entertainment and seat quality are superior to their competitors. As a consequence, even though it charges a premium price, its key offerings are at an even higher premium and therefore it offers to customers a superior value proposition. Figure 6.2 provides a visual illustration of this superior value proposition.

FIGURE 6.2. SUPERIOR VALUE PROPOSITION

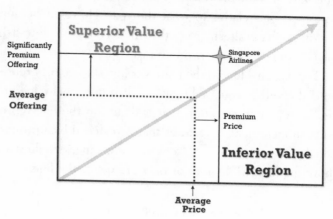

Components of an Employee Value Proposition

This simple tool and framework can also be used to evaluate the superiority or inferiority of a company's value proposition to *employees* and therefore determine the extent to which the firm is likely to succeed in attracting and retaining the numbers and quality of talent it desires.

Like customers, employees pay a price to work for a company. This sentence and perspective almost always strikes executives, especially HR executives, as strange. Often, they say to me, "No, you've got it backwards. We pay employees; they don't pay us." However, my research clearly shows that from employees' perspectives, they pay a price to work for a given company and that perceived price varies from one company to another. So what prices do employees pay? Employees pay a price in terms of hours they spend on the job or thinking, worrying or fretting about the job when they are away. They pay a price in terms of the time they spend away from home while traveling for the job. They pay a price in terms of the effort, energy and talent they give to the job and company. They pay a price in terms of the stress they endure or the extent to which they concentrate and focus during the day. They pay a price in terms of the blood, sweat and tears they give on the company's behalf.

So what do employees get for the price they pay? As with products and services, companies have specific features that constitute their employment offerings. While most executives immediately think of money as the most important feature of an employment offering, my research and that of others has consistently demonstrated that while money is important, it is not the only thing employees care about. Taken together, the research indicates that there are four general buckets of things employees care about and what we might term the categories of the employment offering: company, leadership, job and rewards.

Company. This category of the employee offering consists of what the company does (the challenges it tackles) and how it does it (its values and culture). These elements of the employment offering are important parts of the "deal" employees get in exchange for the price they pay in blood, sweat and tears. Like the styling or performance of a car, employees are willing to pay a price for features of a company that they value, including its reputation, its culture and the contribution it makes to the world. As with customers, not all employees value a given feature of a company in the same way. Therefore, it is possible that for a certain set of employees, the company's grand reputation counts for very little, while for employees of a different profile, the company's reputation counts for quite a lot.

Leadership. The quality of the company's leaders and their ability to identify and develop future leaders are also key features of a company's employment offering. Virtually everyone has to work for a leader and a company's ability to identify and develop good leaders directly affects the quality of work life of employees. Do leaders care about employees? Do they spend time coaching and developing employees? To the extent that employees answer "yes" to these and other related questions, the quality of the leadership aspect of the company's EVP goes up.

Job. The job is a third part of the employment offering. Specifically, how interesting or exciting the job is, the freedom and challenge it involves, and the growth it provides the employee are the most salient features of the job. Essentially, this element of the EVP focuses on the extent to which the job offers employees the opportunity to do well and feel good about what they do today and what they can do tomorrow are important parts of the job in the EVP. As a consequence, the extent to which the resources and tools they need to do their best are provided are also important parts of the job in the EVP.

Rewards. The fourth and final category is the one on which we most often focus. As anyone would suspect, direct and indirect financial rewards are important to employees. In most cases, however, financial rewards are means to other ends. They provide employees with the opportunity to take care of their personal and family needs (e.g., housing, food, clothing). Financial rewards are also means to other desires such as status or ego needs (e.g., a big house or fancy car). They can be a means to desired activities (e.g., sailing, skiing, relaxing, traveling). In fact, it is the versatility of money as a means to other desired ends that makes it so powerful. Consequently, direct and nondirect financial rewards are always an important part of the reward category of any company's employment offering. However, career prospects and development opportunities are also key rewards as are social rewards, such as praise,

FIGURE 6-3. DIMENSIONS OF THE EMPLOYEE VALUE PROPOSITION

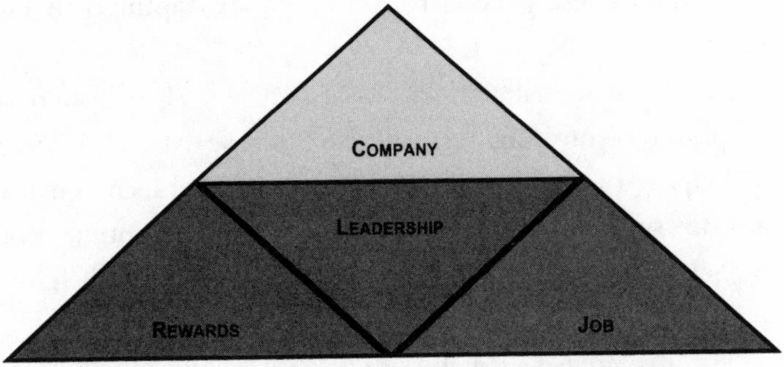

recognition and the opportunity to interact with people employees enjoy.

Taken together, these four categories of the employment offering constitute most of what employees assess in determining whether the price they pay is getting them a superior or inferior value.

Employee Value Propositions in Asia

Over the last three years I have collected data from nearly 7,000 employees across 14 countries in Asia in order to test the true power of a superior Employee Value Proposition. The results of those empirical analyses demonstrate two important conclusions. First, the general strength or weakness of a firm's EVP is a very strong predictor of critical outcomes such as employee commitment, employee extra effort and employee intent to leave or stay with the com-pany. While not explicitly examined in this research, past research has clearly demonstrated that employee commitment and extra effort are important drivers of employee performance and that employees' intent to stay or leave a company is the most proximate predictor of actual employee turnover.[2] These general relationships are captured in Figure 6.4.

As Figure 6.4 illustrates, an attractive EVP will increase employee commitment. It will also increase extra effort, such as helping out other employees even though such activities are not spelled out in the employee's job description. Both higher employee commitment and extra effort will have a positive impact on employee performance.

An attractive EVP will decrease an employee's intent to leave the company. Obviously, the higher the employee's intent to leave, the more likely they will leave, which will in turn have a negative impact on performance.

Theoretical relationships are fine, especially when they are based on past empirical studies, but what do the empirical results of my studies in Asia show? Figure 6.5 illustrates the actual empirical relationships but interpreting the results without the use of statistics requires some explanation.

First, it is important to appreciate that all the relationships were in the predicted direction and all of them were statistically significant. The "+" or "−" sign in front of the

FIGURE 6-4. IMPACT OF EVP

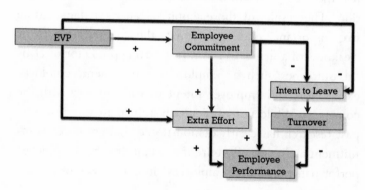

FIGURE 6-5. EFFECTS OF EVP IN ASIA

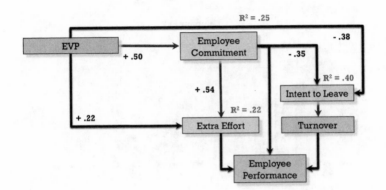

numbers in Figure 6.5 tells you the direction of the relationship. The number after the "+" or "−" sign tells you the strength of the relationship based on a regression analysis. A number between .25 and .50 indicates a strong empirical relationship.

Second, the number after the R^2 tells you how much of the variation in that variable is explained by the indicated drivers. For example, EVP explained 25 percent of all the variance in employee commitment, and in combination, EVP and employee commitment explained 40 percent of the variation in employee intent to leave. EVP and employee commitment in combination explained 22 percent of all the variation in extra effort. Not only are all these results statistically significant, but in the context of social science research, they are quite strong.

There are other ways to help illustrate the quantitative power of having a strong versus weak Employee Value Proposition. Figure 6.6 shows the composite EVP for a set of companies in the study that had at least 200 employees who participated in the research. As you can see, there was

FIGURE 6-6. DISTRIBUTION OF COMPANY COMPOSITE EVP SCORES

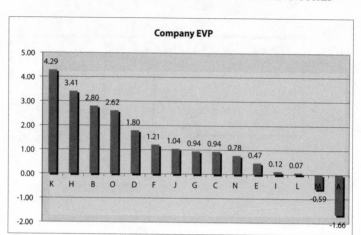

a fair bit of variation in the composite EVP. The highest company (Company K) had an EVP of 4.29 and the weakest had a negative EVP of −1.66 (Company A). Although the exact algorithm for computing the composite EVP is not critical for our purposes here, it is important to appreciate what the numbers basically mean. The more positive the EVP number, the more it says that employees feel they are getting great value from the company in terms of the four dimensions (i.e., company, leadership, job and rewards) relative to the price they are paying. EVP numbers close to zero indicate that employees are getting about what they pay for. A negative EVP number indicates that employees feel they are paying more than they are getting.

It is important to keep one last thing in mind when it comes to positive or negative EVP numbers. Positive numbers do not mean that those companies have the highest absolute values in terms of company, leadership, job and reward scores. Positive numbers mean that these companies have the highest relative values. In other words, employees feel that relative to what they are paying, they are getting a lot. Conversely, negative numbers do not mean that those companies have the lowest absolute values in terms of company, leadership, job and reward scores. Negative numbers mean that these companies have the lowest relative values or that employees feel that relative to what they are paying, they are not getting much in return.

Figure 6.7 helps us visually appreciate the relationship between a company's composite EVP score and the likelihood that employees will leave the company. As illustrated, the higher the EVP score, the lower the intent to leave (or conversely, the higher the intent to stay). The diagonal line essentially shows the perfect trend line, which in turn makes it easy to visually see how close the actual data points are to a perfect relationship. As is evident, the actual data points are very close to falling exactly on the trend line.

FIGURE 6-7. RELATIONSHIP BETWEEN COMPANY EVP AND EMPLOYEE INTENT TO LEAVE

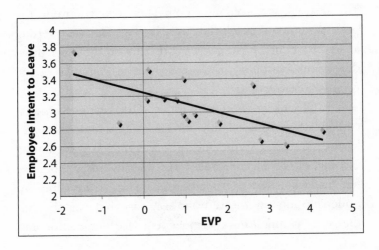

EVP Variation

Even though the composite EVP had a significant impact on employee commitment, extra effort, and intent to leave or stay with the firm, it was not the case that every company with a superior EVP had high scores on all four dimensions (company, leadership, job and rewards) or that every company with an inferior EVP had low scores on every dimension. In many cases, companies that had a strong composite EVP had average or above average on most dimensions but had outstanding scores on one or two dimensions.

In some cases, this configuration was deliberate. For example, one of the companies in the study had only an average score on rewards on purpose. Because they are a relatively labor-intensive business, they did not want to increase their labor cost relative to the market by paying premium wages. Their scores on leadership and job were somewhat above average, but their scores on company (especially company culture) were among some of the highest scores in the entire study. Furthermore, their employees felt that they were paying an average price in terms of hours, stress, sacrifice, and so on. Therefore, relative to the price the employees felt they were paying, they were getting a fantastic value on company, good value on the other three dimensions, resulting in a strong overall composite value proposition to employees.

Let us look at another example. One of the high-tech companies scored slightly above average on company, leadership and rewards, but its scores on job were among the highest of all companies. In other words, employees felt that what they were getting in terms of the company, leadership and rewards were above average, but what they felt they were getting from their jobs (e.g., freedom, autonomy, excitement, challenge) were exceptional. Interestingly, upon further analysis, it was clear that these employees valued the job dimension more than the other three. To be clear, employees at this company valued all four dimensions, but they cared most about the job dimension. The fact that this company scored the highest and was among the highest scores in the entire study meant that employees in this company were getting more of what they valued most.

However, it is important to keep in mind the impact of price. As stated earlier, value is NOT in what you get, it is in what you get relative to what you feel you paid. As an illustration of this, one of the other high-tech companies in the study also had a very high score on job and average or above average scores on the other three dimensions. However, the company's composite EVP was not high and its employees did not score well on employee commitment or extra effort and were more likely to leave. What was the problem? The problem was that employees felt they were paying a very high price for what they were getting. They felt they were working significantly longer hours, enduring more stress, sacrificing more personal and family needs, and so on. As a consequence, just as customers are not likely to become repeat buyers if they feel they are not getting value for money, these employees were much less likely to remain with the company and were actively looking for alternative employment.

Conclusion

What can we make of all this? For an executive, I think there are seven key "take aways" from this chapter:

1. **Shift in Power.** A shift in the basis of competition, information asymmetry, firm-specific benefits and

supply and demand have all shifted the balance of power away from employers and towards employees.

2. **20-year War for Talent.** These four shifts are not temporary or reversible in the near or medium term. They are likely to be in force, especially in Asia, for another 20 years, which means that despite the current economic downturn, the war for talent will rage in Asia for a long time to come.

3. **What You Offer Matters.** What employees feel they get from the company, its leadership, the job and rewards matter. These four categories capture about 80 percent of what employees care about.

4. **Price Matters.** Like customers, employees do not just care about what they get, they also care about what they have to pay for what they get. Employees pay attention to the price they pay to work for a company in terms of hours, stress, sacrifice, blood, sweat and tears and that calculus affects their overall sense of value of the employment proposition.

5. **Configuration Matters.** A winning EVP does not need to have superior value across all four EVP offering dimensions equally. A superior EVP can come from average or above average offering on some dimensions as long as there is an outstanding offering on the remaining dimensions that are not offset by a high price.

6. **Matching Matters.** The most powerful EVP configuration is when the highest offering is provided on the dimension(s) that employees value the most. Therefore, knowing the type of employees you want to attract and retain, understanding what they value most, and matching your EVP to those criteria will yield the greatest Return on Investment (ROI).

7. **EVP Drives Key Outcomes.** A superior EVP is not just a nice thing to do for people but has direct and indirect effects on outcomes such as employee turnover and performance that directly affect overall business outcomes. Therefore, line executives, not just HR managers, need to measure, monitor and enhance their Employee Value Proposition.

At the end of the day, the truth (even if it is inconvenient) is that people are a company's most important asset and the balance of power has shifted towards employees. They have greater competitive value, easier ability to know their value, lower switching costs and higher demand than ever before. Companies that recognize this and executives who proactively seek to measure, monitor and enhance their Employee Value Proposition will be the ones who not only wage and win the war for talent but also the battles for competitive position.

Endnotes

1. Farrell, D. & Grant, A., "China's Looming Talent Shortage," *McKinsey Quarterly*, November 2005.
2. Mowday, R. T., Porter, L. W. & Steers, R. M., *Employee-Organization Linkages: The Psychology of Commitment, Absenteeism and Turnover* (New York: Academic Press, 1982); Steers, R. M., Porter, L. W. & Bigley, G. A., *Motivation and Leadership at Work*, 6th ed. (New York: McGraw-Hill, 1996).

CHAPTER 7

The Right Leaders in Place in Asia . . . The Right Future Leaders in the Pipeline

Peter Smith

Overview

The need to identify, develop and hold the right leadership in Asia is, if anything, even more essential in these challenging times. In this paper, we look at six strategies aimed at ensuring that organizations have the right leaders in place and a strong pipeline of battle-ready future leaders.

1. Change gears on your leadership model
2. Reduce the prevalence of "single-issue" managers
3. Place greater emphasis on leadership achievements
4. Push for more acute, accurate segmentation and differentiation of talent
5. Attend to your best talent as individually as you focus on your "AAA" clients
6. Require your current executives to be great leaders of talent

Introduction

Asia has demonstrated tremendous economic growth over the last decade, emerging as an increasingly visible player on the world stage. As a result, we have also seen the rise of corporate Asia, with some of the region's leading organizations not only growing larger in size, but becoming more innovative, ambitious and global in scale and presence, with several Asian companies targeting acquisitions both in the region and beyond.

However, by late 2008, the aftershocks from the global financial crisis (GFC) originating in the West began to impact the rest of the world, including Asia. However, not all Asian countries have been affected in the same way. For example, Hong Kong, Japan, Korea and Singapore are technically in recession, yet Indonesia, China and India are still growing, despite facing significant economic slowdown.

To date, individual nations in Asia have responded to the crisis with level-headed, pragmatic measures to limit its impact on their economies. The measures put in place vary greatly depending on country-specific circumstances and the resources available. China, Japan, Singapore, South Korea, Taiwan and Malaysia have all announced fiscal packages of more than 4 percent of GDP for 2009, twice as large as America's stimulus this year.[1] As a result of the boost from the government's stimulus efforts, China's growth expectations have improved, with the World Bank raising its 2009 economic growth forecast to 7.2 percent.[2]

Governments are also devising innovative ways to stimulate growth, limit impact on people and prepare for the future. In Singapore, for example, the government introduced the Skills Program for Upgrading and Resilience, or SPUR. SPUR encourages companies affected by declining business to retain workers by sending them for training, as opposed to retrenching them. This aims to help employers save manpower costs and better manage their excess manpower during the downturn, while upgrading their workers to strengthen business competitiveness for the upturn. At the same time, SPUR helps local employees to develop skills and seek new employment opportunities. Overall, SPUR aims to develop capabilities at a national level in order to be better prepared for the recovery.

Asian organizations are also undertaking specific actions to cope with the downturn and stimulate growth. Many hardest hit Asian companies are the traditional low-cost exporters catering to North American and European economies. Although some were already looking to expand beyond these markets, the downturn has hastened and spread this intent. As a result, some organizations have begun looking for alternative consumer and resource markets in promising Asian, African, Middle Eastern and South American geographies. For example, the Malaysian petroleum giant, Petronas, is armed with financial reserves and is potentially expanding into Africa, Central Asia and Southeast Asia.[3] In addition, companies are seeking to compete more directly with European and American Asian companies.

Besides the move to new consumer and resource markets, Asian organizations are tapping into new talent markets. A leading Indian IT services firm is leveraging the downturn as an opportunity to move up the value chain. In particular, the company is now able to attract quality consulting talent from premium firms in developed markets such as the United States, which was a difficult proposition even just a year ago. Of course, the challenge and ultimate success will lie in the company's ability to retain this talent once the US economy recovers.

It is clear that while these are challenging times for Asia, they present an unprecedented opportunity for the region to take center stage in driving recovery and growth. To quote remarks made at the recent World Economic Forum on East Asia, "There is no doubt that the global financial crisis has accelerated the shift in economic power from the West towards Asia . . . And Asia in a sense needs to step up now and play the role such power brings."[4]

This role demands substantial leadership capability. However, even before the financial crisis, Asian companies were facing a leadership shortage. Since the 2005 McKinsey & Company study on the War for Talent, there have been questions about the availability of leadership talent in Asia. The report stated, "Given the global aspirations of many Chinese companies, over the next 10–15 years they will need 75,000 leaders who can work effectively in global environments; today they have only 3,000–5,000."[5] Aging populations in the more developed Asian countries are likely to exacerbate leadership problems and need to be accounted for in leadership plans.

"An army is easy to raise; a general to lead them is hard to find," said Ma Zhi Yuan,[6] and these words still ring true in Asia. The key item on the talent management agenda, then, is what can proactively be done to develop the right leaders—leaders who can rise to the challenges facing Asian companies today and in the future.

This means organizations in Asia must attract and develop the right quantity and quality of leadership talent; retain this talent, particularly mid-career talent; attract private sector entrants to key government roles; invest in leadership training and development; commit to developing leadership depth and breadth and hotwire the ability to deal with change in the organization. The following constitutes a set of proposed solutions to meet these objectives.

Change Gears on the Leadership Model

When faced with a crisis, organizations often turn to established leaders who have a solid foundation in the fundamentals of their business operations and demonstrate a strong system of traditional values such as integrity, professionalism and agility. This attempt to reframe leadership in more traditional terms may be summarized in the words of Australian songwriter Peter Allen, "Let's go backwards . . . 'cause forward failed."

Nowhere is this more evident than in the very epicenter of the current global financial crisis—banks and other financial institutions. These erstwhile bastions of mega deal-makers and traders are now turning to operational, balanced and execution-oriented leaders—those who can weed out the toxic assets, strengthen the balance sheet and make the nuts and bolts of banking work again.

If the period before the global financial crisis was characterized by managing the "upside of risk," the meltdown has demanded from our organizations the maturity to manage the "downside of risk," which has spurred a new balance in assessing leadership profiles and subsequently making key appointment decisions. While the ability to grow a business and leverage risk is no less important, leadership profiles are again emphasizing that a leader must also lead with uncompromising attention to sustainability, robustness and governance; and must demand and live the traditional values of integrity, professionalism and agility.

A large industrial conglomerate in Thailand recently redefined its core values. Not surprisingly, integrity and professionalism were adopted as two of the core corporate values. Going further, the organization realized that employees needed support to interpret and apply the values in their individual context. Accordingly, a series of communication and training initiatives were undertaken to illustrate work behaviors expected from leaders as well as employees. The efforts to drive their values did not stop here. To truly drive the adoption of these values, they were integrated into the company's core management processes. For example, the value of integrity was embodied in the code of conduct and delegation of authority, as well as being an integral part of the company's leadership competencies, talent assessment and development programs.

In another example, a statutory board in Singapore embedded its core values into its performance management system. This enables the acknowledgment of leaders who display these values through performance assessments, incentives, salary increments and career opportunities. Similarly, a large regional consumer goods company is working to replace its traditional merit increase program with a system whereby demonstrated skills tied to values are the key driver of pay increases. This is in support of efforts to change the culture of the company. In the CEO's own words, "We need to change the spirit around here."

It is also important to highlight that a number of companies have never let go of their focus on sustainability and values. One such company, a leading Indian conglomerate, considers sustainable growth in each of its diverse businesses as a key expectation from leadership. Accordingly, board reviews of this listed organization go beyond quarterly or even annual performance targets; rather, the review takes a long-term perspective and examines the sustainability of strategies and operations. The assessment of leaders is based on informed judgment, and rewards are based on "how" performance results are achieved. An alternative approach used by a Singapore company involves assigning leaders to a position for longer than the normal high potential posting—at least four years, which ensures they are clearly responsible for both "what" and "how" results are achieved.

Asia has experienced several crises in recent times: SARS, the dot-com bust and the Asian financial crisis of 1997. The management of these crises has allowed business and political leaders to be better prepared this time around, and also take a longer-term view of decisions. Combined with knowledge of the talent shortages faced in precrisis times, leaders are more focused on retaining employment than in the typical Western model, which moves more quickly to reduce staff in a downturn.

Leadership Models Going Forward—A Change of Gears

Moving away from:
- ✗ Obsessively chasing the upside of risk
- ✗ Unsustainable gearing and leverage limits
- ✗ Marginalizing people as commodities

Moving back towards:
- ✓ Sustainability; robustness; governance
- ✓ Traditional values—integrity; professionalism; agility
- ✓ Traditional experiences—cross-cultural/cross-divisional

Leading to more sustainable balance

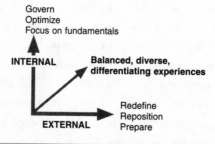

Reduce the Prevalence of "Single-Issue" Managers

Another foundation of leadership success in Asia today is the imperative to form future leaders through cross-cultural and cross-divisional experiences. Many clients in different industries cite this as a key principle for charting development paths of their future leaders. For example, a leading consumer goods company in the region has a model which explicitly specifies that nobody can be appointed to a top leadership position without at least one out-of-country experience and one out-of-division exposure. A similar policy was echoed by a global chemical manufacturer and an ASEAN-based supply-chain provider, clearly reflecting its appeal across industries. Some governments also follow a similar philosophy towards grooming leaders. In Singapore, officers are evaluated annually on their ability to work across government entities and routinely posted to a variety of roles and organizations as part of the succession planning process.

Emerging Asian organizations have quickly adopted the idea of "complete leaders" groomed through diverse experiences. A case in point, one Asian *Fortune* 500 state-owned enterprise in China was keen to expand from its traditional trading capabilities to other industries and businesses. However, to implement this strategy, the firm realized it needed "comprehensive and complete leaders" with portable leadership skills and industry knowledge. This implied identifying leaders who not only had a strong grasp of their own business, but also demonstrated substantial understanding of other businesses. This understanding had to be developed by providing opportunities for exposure, interaction and possible experience in diverse industries.

In another instance, a technology-focused client in the Indian biosciences industry realized that top-notch scientists alone were insufficient to support its growth strategy. It needed more comprehensive talent in the form of "scientist-leaders" who could demonstrate both technical expertise and leadership competencies. The organization then embarked on a two-year program to identify the specific leadership competencies desired and development interventions for its scientists.

However, this approach of building leaders through an orchestrated management of their career experiences faces some unique challenges in Asia. Particularly, in high-growth economies such as India and China, companies find it difficult to grow leaders at the same pace as their organization is expanding. The traditional model of developing leaders over a ten-year or longer time horizon is often deemed too slow in creating the required pipeline. This problem is exacerbated by a relatively small pool of potential leadership talent and relatively high attrition rates. Moreover, as Asian companies expand overseas, they rapidly require a set of leaders capable of managing global and complex organizations.

One answer is to "buy" talent, a strategy which worked well for the West for many years. However, the challenges in Asia are greater in terms of the diversity of languages and cultures. Therefore, for many companies, the answer lies in accelerated leadership development. While this may sound counterintuitive to our initial premise, it is in fact an implementation of the same intent that delivers faster results. Accelerated leadership development requires a significant investment of resources in a compressed time period and commitment from top management.

A leading bank in India showcases this approach. On the back of India's economic growth and reforms, this bank grew rapidly, as did its workforce, which increased almost tenfold in the period from 2002 to 2008. This growth necessitated a rapid increase in the population of middle managers, often through promotion and the appointment of underprepared talent. The result was a large number of middle managers, most of whom lacked the experience and capabilities to effectively lead their teams. Moreover, owing to significant growth pressures, it was difficult to invest time in developing this pool for further movement into leadership positions.

At this juncture, the bank faced a critical choice in appointing its leaders: buy talent from the market or develop this pool of middle managers. It chose to proactively invest in developing its internal talent for leadership positions. This decision was made based on an economic analysis of the *build* versus *buy* strategy and the longer-term vision to establish a sustainable leadership pipeline. The decision resulted in the implementation of an accelerated leadership strategy and compressed learning paths.

An American semiconductor company faced a similar situation in India with the same results: accelerated development was instrumental in maintaining the pace of growth and quality of output of its India R&D operations.[7] This illustrates the benefits of developing rather than buying your leadership talent. The latter may be a tempting option for many Asian firms, particularly in the "buyer's" labor market that typically follows an economic downturn. It is also true that organizations are usually able to create more opportunities for high-potential and high-value employees in an economic boom; however, those opportunities may be reduced in troubled times. Indeed, many promised opportunities to move and grow within the organization may not even be fulfilled. What is needed is an unwavering commitment to leadership development that holds steady through testing times.

Place Greater Emphasis on Leadership Achievements

While emphasizing core values, leading companies are simultaneously moving back to stability, sustainability, robustness, governance, risk management and clear accountability. This is particularly true in the newfound commitment to key metrics (both financial and nonfinancial) to complement the change in leadership and vision.

The economic turbulence, coupled with the large amount of press received by what many considered to be excessive pay packages, has driven many companies to reconsider their Key Performance Indicators (KPIs) towards more holistic measures such as economic profit. In addition, new plans around the region are sprouting up with different overall objectives: more towards tactical measures and less about growth. And given the constraints in budgets, remuneration committees are becoming more selective about who is awarded shares but are very willing to provide awards to those identified as key executives, or key risks, if there is a strong enough business case.

One recent trend in the West that has not yet reached Asia is the introduction of claw-back provisions on deferred compensation plans meant to ensure the sustainability of results. Another global trend that is likely to reach Asia soon is the tracking of performance against relative measures comparing against industry competitors or market indices. Both of these would increase the accountability leaders have over short- and long-term results.

Another opportunity presented by the current environment is the ability to get performance distribution right. Human Resource VPs in the region often complain that the "tough" conversations about low performance are even more difficult in Asia given the cultural contexts. However, in tough times, the ability to differentiate good performers is also even more critical, as well as the ability to provide adequate incentives, training opportunities or other means to engage and retain them. One of the leading regional Asian companies, headquartered in Singapore, has decided to tie the number of "good" performers to the results of the unit they belong to. In this way, they are creating a direct link between expected behaviors and expected results.

Push for More Acute, Accurate Segmentation and Differentiation of Talent

Many employers state in their annual reports and other public instances that, "All our employees are our talent" and many claim that the values of equity and merit preclude an explicit approach to talent management. However, the harsh reality is that if all employees receive the same standard of nurturing and development, then the process will result in sparse and ineffective treatment of employees. In mature organizations, talent segmentation represents a way to move beyond one-size-fits-all thinking in the shaping of performance, development and retention prac-tices. Talent segmentation is a strategic approach that can help organizations identify distinct talent segments and then apply different talent management practices to each segment.

By segmenting talent more accurately, successful organizations can avoid the pitfalls of commoditization and reallocate resources from low-value to high-value segments to drive business success.

The Thai industrial conglomerate mentioned earlier in this chapter has an interesting approach to driving acute differentiation of talent. This company owns close to 30 different companies across the value chain, grouped into four separate divisions by product group. The management recognizes that each segment operates differently, and a one-size-fits-all approach towards talent identification would not serve the needs of any segment. Accordingly, each segment leadership is empowered to define its own criteria to identify its leaders. The only common requirement from each segment is to include common core values in the selection criteria.

A successful approach to talent differentiation requires, at a minimum, that organizations manage employees in terms of four potentially competing perspectives:

- Who are the established and future leaders that you need to **retain and grow**?

  - These are individuals who are the focus of the talent process and whom the company wants to retain. They have significant capabilities and are potentially critical for the business.

- Are there any groups of established and future leaders that need to be treated differently because they **add a disproportionate amount of value**?

  - Expatriate leaders
  - Particular technical skill experience that is essential for success, e.g., geologists in an oil gas company; leaders with experience in acquisitions; or leaders who have established business operations in a new geographical location. For example, a Singaporean logistics business established a "dedicated

launch team" to ensure consistency in processes and culture as they expanded geographically. The leaders of this launch team added significant value to the firm and as such were recognized for their contribution.

- Who are the current effective and solid performers that you need to *engage and develop*?
  - Encourage line managers to keep an eye on these individuals and provide them with opportunities to develop and demonstrate their capabilities.
- Who are the marginal and poor performers (or incongruent performers from a values basis) who you need to *manage and resolve*?
  - Look closely at these individuals to determine the cause of their poor performance, which could include a poor fit with role or organization, unclear expectations, a need for additional training or development (i.e., coaching), or a lack of capability.

Attend to Your Best Talent as Individually as You Focus on Your "AAA" Clients

It is rare to find an organization that has not benefited from adopting a systematic process for managing its customers. Popularly known as Customer Relationship Management (CRM), this process aims to identify critical customer segments, focus on customized strategies for each segment and ultimately create "sticky" relationships based on an intimate, personalized knowledge of top customers. In many ways, this approach translates directly to the talent management process.

At the heart of great customer management is the development of a strong, robust *relationship*—an equally important (yet all too often missing) ingredient and differentiator in great talent management.

In practice, this means that organizations need to track talent early and keep them close. It requires an early commitment to stretching lateral movement that builds the qualities and values of great leaders. The differentiator is the depth and resilience of the relationship—how sticky it is. That may not necessarily be with the supervisor, but it should be with a "significant" representative of the organization.

Often this representative may even be the CEO. An interesting illustration of this approach is the group managing director and CEO of leading global supply-chain company Olam International, Sunny George Verghese. Verghese realized that the success of the business depended upon grooming "entrepreneurial" leaders who understand and share his vision, have a deep knowledge of the company's operations and demonstrate capability to break ground in new markets or product lines. High-caliber managers were identified across the world to form an elite team, and this group was then treated as special and given personal attention and frequent trainings by the MD himself. No new business is initiated without a member of this team first going in to set up operations and establish the culture. Most of these elite team members have since been made shareholders in the company, which is listed on the Singapore Stock Exchange. This move was designed to further instill the sense of entrepreneurial ownership among key talent.[8]

An Indian firm applied this principle of treating top talent "individually" in a slightly different manner, taking the approach deeper into the organization by identifying future leaders at the junior- and middle-management levels and instituting them as a "shadow board." As shadow board members, these high-potential young employees have an opportunity to comment on the annual strategy and company performance, which exposes them to the company's strategy and firm-wide operations, the CEO and management committee, and their decision-making processes. As Mercer's *What's Working* survey[9] shows, Indian employees highly value such opportunities regarding the kind of work they get to do and the impact they feel they can make.

Organizations pivot around a core group of critical human assets—their most valuable players—who require solutions tailored to their needs, concerns, risks and pressures. The contributions and expectations of your highest-performing leaders justify an investment in the creation and delivery of personalized approaches to their retention, development and engagement.

There are many other successful practices for differentiating talent ranging from mentorship programs to special assignments and recognition programs. However, the most successful all rest on a simple set of principles: be thorough and relentless in assessing your top talent, and once you know who they are, treat each of them as a very special asset, even if it means differential treatment from the rest. From a talent management perspective, this could include implementing a higher pay philosophy for key talent, retention bonuses and share grants, access to top-level training and external coaches or other means to ensure that these employees not only stay with the company but also continue to grow.

Require Your Current Executives to Be Great Leaders of Talent

There is no easy way to win the war for your most valuable talent, and before you do, you will first need to win the battle for your executives' time and attention. Harnessing their influence, creativity, active support and problem-solving prowess is key to solving your retention and development challenges on a sustained basis. It is also important to make it clear that talent development is one of their top priorities. In fact, many boards now periodically assess risk from a talent perspective and many companies find their plans thwarted by lack of sufficient talent. As the regional MD of a supply-chain company said recently, "The main reason our company has not grown even faster in Asia Pacific is that we do not have in the company the people who can manage the next large account."

The key to transforming busy, easily distracted executives into creative leaders is a talent summit, which combines insightful data and informed decision-support tools with an executive team's knowledge, authority and creativity. This all adds up to ensure that the best possible high-impact, high-priority talent and succession decisions are made.

This summit is invariably the "tipping point" at which the momentum for action becomes unstoppable. However, it is the actions arising from the summit which will differentiate organizations which merely "talk" from those which are truly "great leaders of talent." These actions may range from one-to-one relationship discussions with key talent, investment-driven job moves and committed leadership development programs. The "right" set of actions may vary for each organization; the two cases which follow serve to illustrate this.

One of Australia's largest industrial and retail conglomerates bring their diverse business leaders together twice a year to review the bench strength of their current leaders as well as the strengths and weaknesses of their leadership pipeline. Their summit agenda focuses equally on strategic initiatives as well as tactical responses and leverages a "community of leaders" to consolidate opinions and creatively solve the challenge of retaining their best people and effectively building a strong pipeline to fill key roles across the group. While individual succession planning plays its part for business critical positions, broader job-family pipeline management has successfully replaced traditional succession management for the majority of middle and senior roles. In addition to being the "taxi-rank" for appointments across the group, it also highlights endemic development gaps and areas of weakness that might necessitate a "buy" rather than "build" response. The summit is sponsored by the group CEO and is an essential part of the C-Suite annual business agenda.

With its roots in its partnership culture, a financial services multinational operating in Asia leverages the creative talents and experience of its executives in what they call their promotion roundtable. Rather than traditional succession management, their roundtable process has a strong focus on merit and long-term retention. It aims at promoting its best talent at the right time in their career journey and gives the business a great chance of recognizing and retaining its people for their contributions and potential. Using sophisticated decision-support software developed by Mercer, their promotion model identifies regional staff ready for consideration using a promotion algorithm that includes specific behaviors for success, accomplishments and performance, key position attributes, professional experience, total years of experience and time in title.

Conclusion

Great talent management requires a "community" of executives, not just single chains of command, to engage in a shared accountability for the actions essential to fuel growth and manage risk. This should include strong "by example" ownership and leadership action from the CEO. The following three examples illustrate Asian success stories. While all three examples span different industries, countries and situations, a common theme of top management commitment to developing leadership talent exists. (See box on pages 150–151 for China case study.)

Doosan is a leading South Korean business conglomerate, which has seen success in its global ambitions and growth strategies despite crises and setbacks in the past. In 2007, Doosan Infracore, the group's construction-equipment arm, staged the biggest ever foreign acquisition by a South Korean company. Its success in globalizing is credited to the Chairman, Y. M. Park's approach towards instilling some of the most progressive business and leadership development programs across the organization. In his words, "When I started to redo the HR system, I said we're going to be a global company and people are going to be the centerpiece, so we would invest heavily in improving our people's skills. I wanted to create a system good enough to support a global company."[10]

Infosys Technologies Ltd. was started in India in 1981 by seven people with US$250. Today, it is a global leader in next-generation IT and consulting with revenues of over US$4 billion. The organization's emphasis on talent management is indicated by the opening quote of its 2007–08

Annual Report, in which chairman and chief mentor N. R. Narayana Murthy states, "Our core assets walk out every evening. It is our duty to make sure these assets return the next morning, mentally and physically enthusiastic and energetic."[11] Aptly entitled "Power of Talent," the report goes on to detail initiatives undertaken to develop leaders including the Infosys Leadership Institute (ILI). ILI caters to employees' needs in the areas of behavioral and leadership skills and supports personal development through systematic processes. ILI's efforts resulted in 180,019 training days in fiscal year 2007–08 alone.

Mercer's "Leading Through Unprecedented Times" study in Asia[12] showed that companies are experiencing difficulty finding key talent with the right mix of skills and experience to fit their organization. In addition, respondents expressed that they prefer building talent from within the organization rather than buying from the market, which puts added pressure on the company's internal systems to identify key talent. Successful companies are taking active steps to manage and retain their key talent in an effort to be ready for growth opportunities once the market turbulence subsides.

Talent remains in short supply in the world's fastest growing region and companies that do not have a sustainable and long-term leadership strategy to build, retain and engage the leadership pipeline may be unable to fuel future growth.

Identifying Talent Through Audits: Case Study of a Chinese Financial Institution

Situation
- Regional Chinese financial institution
- More than 1,000 employees
- Ambitious to quickly expand its business scale
- Significant competition in traditional markets and products from other financial institutions
- New business strategy launched to meet the demands of the market
- Significant shareholding by foreign bank has resulted in a focus upon transforming the business, including the approach to human capital management

Challenges
- The business strategy requires a new skill set in the organization, in particular, the business and people management skills and behaviors
- The executive and management group comprises employees with vastly differing levels of management experience
- Limited international business experience in the existing executive and management team

Actions
- Define expected levels of skills and behaviors required for success by executives and managers against international "best-in-class" behaviors
- To gain an in-depth understanding of the leadership skills compared with the expected requirement, design and run a one-day assessment center for 120 executives and managers within a very short timeframe

- Customized design of assessment activities to be appropriate for the business and cultural context
- Provide individual feedback reports and one-on-one feedback sessions to reinforce development priorities for each executive and manager

Results
- The core strengths and development priorities of the executive and management group were identified
- Key future leaders identified
- Leadership development programs recommended to be redesigned to support the development of the skill and behavior gaps identified by the assessment center
- An annual process was put in place which allowed for the integration of performance management, talent assessments and succession planning

Endnotes

1. "Crouching Tigers: Asia's Economies," *The Economist*, May 13, 2009.
2. "China Quarterly Update," World Bank, June 2009.
3. "Petronas Poised for More International Expansion to Further Diversify Businesses," *Bernama*, December 3, 2008.
4. Group CEO, Standard Chartered Bank, speaking at the World Economic Forum on East Asia.
5. Farrell, D. & Grant, A., "China's Looming Talent Shortage," *McKinsey Quarterly*, November 2005.
6. A celebrated Chinese playwright during the Yuan Dynasty (1271–1368).
7. Diez, Fermin, *WorldAtWork Journal*, 2nd Quarter, 2009.
8. "Power to the People," *The Peak*, Singapore, February 2009.
9. "What's Working" Survey, *Mercer India*, 2006.
10. Barton, D. & Deutsch, C., "Transforming a South Korean *Chaebol*: An Interview with Doosan's Yongmaan Park," *McKinsey Quarterly*, September 2008.
11. Infosys Technologies, Annual Report, 2007–08.
12. "Leading Through Unprecedented Times," Global survey, Version 2.0, *Mercer*, June 2009.

CHAPTER 8

Building People

Liew Mun Leong

Introduction

As Asian companies globalize their operations, a key imperative for successful growth is the availability of internationally experienced corporate leaders and a strong management bench. Despite a few decades of rapid growth, Asia still faces a dire shortage of CEOs who can manage global companies. In this paper, I will provide some reasons why Asian companies do not nurture enough CEOs to lead their companies. I will also present CapitaLand as a case study of a rapidly growing and internationalizing Asian company that is attempting to provide the right environment to nurture human capital and groom CEOs.

Insights on Asian Companies' Human Capital Practices

Leadership and human capital development have not been important or urgent features on the corporate agenda for

■ *153* ■

Asian companies until recent years. With the rapid globalization of Asia, these issues will become more pressing if Asian companies are to compete in the global market. In short, Asian companies can no longer treat the development of their human capital and leadership as before.

Why do Asian companies not train or nurture enough CEOs? There are three broad reasons. First, Asian com-panies are late developers in the area of leadership develop-ment. Second, the management in most Asian companies are hampered as the companies are usually either family-owned or state-owned. And lastly, Asian management in multinational companies operating in Asia are not being groomed as CEOs.

Asian Companies Are Relatively Late Developers

Asia lags Western economies in terms of economic and market development. Most Asian countries had "command" or "protectionist" economies. Communist China began to embrace capitalism only three decades ago. Vietnam even more recently. Liberalization of the Indian economy took place only in the early 1990s but remained highly protectionist until a few years ago. Most Asian countries (except for Japan) are still far behind the United States and Europe in terms of per capita GDP. Private enterprises in emerging Asian economies are generally smaller than their counterparts in the West. The only exception was Japan, which has had international companies for several decades. These Japanese companies did provide inspiration for other Asian companies to grow abroad. As a result, it is understandable that Asian companies lag behind their Western counterparts in modernizing their management methods and corporate culture.

Most Major Asian Companies Are Either Family-Owned or State-Owned

Another reason why Asian companies do not nurture corporate leadership is that the majority of enterprises are either family-owned or state-owned. Of the 20 largest Asian listed companies, 13 are family-owned or state-owned. In comparison, of the 20 largest listed companies in the United States and Europe, only two and one are owned by families respectively.[1] Unlike the Western business environment where companies rely or tap on the capital market environment, family- or state-owned enterprises in Asia do not depend on capital markets to grow their operations.

It is inherently not natural for family-owned or state-owned enterprises to develop or groom top-notch corporate business leaders. Family-owned enterprises are typically headed and run by family members. There is less priority or commitment in grooming outsiders into their top management bench. There are some strong entrepreneurial business leaders among the founders of Asian businesses but there are hardly enough corporate business leaders groomed beyond the family tree. Several family-owned enterprises have tried to professionalize their businesses but with limited success as they are not quite prepared or are reluctant to empower outsiders to run independent operations. High-performing executives are rarely posted overseas for exposure as their bosses often want to keep the best by their side to be at their beck and call. These capable executives often also see the merits of staying near the family powerbase lest they be forgotten or sidelined.

On the other hand, state-owned enterprises in many Asian countries are often run by state-appointed leaders and managers who continue to take instructions from the bureaucracy. They are mainly run for the benefit of the state, sometimes with different objectives and often not entirely commercial in objectives and practices. Managers of state-owned enterprises are more often than not former civil servants or politicians who may not have adequate business leadership exposure or training in the current fast-moving commercial world. SOEs generally do not see the need to remunerate state-appointed managers commercial salaries. Neither are they keen to offer competitive salaries to attract outside talents for fear of upsetting the compensation structure within the establishment and creating "morale issues." Many state-owned enterprises are therefore not natural grounds for growing business leaders.

Local Branches of Multinational Corporations Train Managers, Not Leaders

Besides family- and state-owned enterprises, another group of businesses in Asia are the relatively large-scale local branches of multinational companies (MNCs). Until recently, these local branches performed functional management roles or ran specialized functions such as manufacturing, marketing and after-sales support on behalf of Western MNCs. Often, the local leadership in the Asian branches of MNCs may not be fully exposed to the full range of business functions and high-level decision-making processes. Financial authority is also rather limited. Typically, local branches are often guided in their decisions by policies from corporate headquarters back in the West. As such, local leadership are often not bestowed with total accountability and authority available to their counterparts in the West. However, given the weight of Asia in the MNCs' operations in the last decade or so, the situation is improving with more MNCs now localizing their operations.

Having said that, it must be recognized that MNCs do train very good managers, especially functional managers. Some of these MNC-trained managers do subsequently grow into competent CEOs in other companies later on. Several have become entrepreneurs starting up their own companies.

Human Capital Management in CapitaLand

For the above-mentioned reasons, Asia has a dearth of corporate leaders or professional managers who can manage and lead large commercial operations. How then can Asian companies meet the challenges of rapid growth and internationalization?

In the second part of this paper, I will present CapitaLand as a case study on how a rapidly growing and internationalizing company can provide the right environment to nurture human capital and groom future CEOs. Today, CapitaLand has 20 CEOs who are running listed and unlisted companies in the group. Several of them are responsible for multi-geography operations; all of them have balance sheet and profit and loss responsibilities. Eighteen of the 20 CEOs were nurtured in-house.

Background on CapitaLand, an International Real Estate Company

CapitaLand was formed in November 2000 as a result of a merger between government-owned Pidemco Land and publicly listed DBS Land and has Temasek Holdings as its major shareholder (40 percent). While it is often viewed as a partially state-owned enterprise, CapitaLand is completely independent and commercially run by its management. It is supported by a diverse and independent board.[2] Except for corporate governance issues, Temasek does not interfere with CapitaLand's management on its investments, business operations, management appointments or remuneration.

Since its formation, the Group has grown significantly over the last eight years from a Singapore-centric developer into an international real estate group with presence in about 120 cities in over 20 countries. Today, CapitaLand is a multi-sector, multi-geographical real estate company. About 70 percent of CapitaLand's businesses are in Asia. Besides Singapore, the other Asian countries where it has a presence include China, Vietnam, Japan, Thailand, Malaysia, Indonesia, India and Australia. Today, with over 10,000 employees of 95 nationalities, the Group is putting in place a more comprehensive human capital management system to better manage its diverse and growing employee population.

Building People in CapitaLand

CapitaLand places great emphasis on talent management to support its growth rate especially in its international expansion strategy. Indeed, the growth strategy is embodied in the company's credo—"Building People." It has been CapitaLand's maxim for people management from day one. This principle of maximizing the potential of employees underpins the Group's human resource programs on which its growth and success have been built.

The key programs of CapitaLand's human capital management system are fourfold: Attracting Good People, Active Performance Management, Staff Communication and Engagement, and Leadership/Management Training and Development.

Attracting Good People

Recruitment—Not Demand-Driven Only

At CapitaLand, attracting good people into the organization has always been a strategic priority. The Group is always looking out for good people and bringing them in whenever we can find them. Our policy is to recruit continuously, rather than to simply fill vacancies, as we believe that the company would be able to grow and go anywhere with the right people. We believe that when we have the right people, they will build the right business. We therefore take the view that talent recruitment should not be demand-driven. We believe in keeping a "free float" of talent to meet future demand. In any case, real estate is a highly capital-intensive business and the cost of human reserve is relatively small compared to the result of their contribution.

Going for Diversity

To support CapitaLand's growth and promote innovation and creativity, there has been a deliberate effort to build a more diversified employee profile within the Group. To achieve this, we have hired people with varied training and disciplines and from other industries and geographies. Thus, at CapitaLand today, we have employees from 95 different nationalities. This geographical and cultural diversity has enabled us to go international in our real estate business. We also have staff from diverse educational backgrounds, ranging from engineering, finance, economics, accountancy, architecture to history and arts. Within the Group, there is a good mix of young talents, mid-career hires and "silver hairs" to provide a balance of fresh perspectives and experienced views.

In a 2007 McKinsey survey[3] of executives from 93 countries on the global trends that will most affect their companies over the next five years, it was found that the most significant trend—cited by 47 percent of the executives—is the intensifying battle for talented people. To ensure that CapitaLand wins the war for talent, we have an aggressive recruitment program in place to recruit externally from multiple sources. For example, we scout internationally for talents and have established several scholarship programs targeting, but not limited to, young Singaporeans, Malaysians, Chinese, Vietnamese and Indians. We are constantly on the lookout for good people whom we can hire. We also hire senior, mid-career executives from outside to support the Group's rapid growth. We have an Employee Referral Program because we believe that everyone is a talent scout for the company. More importantly, every business CEO is personally involved in the recruitment process, which includes talent identification and selection interviews.

Core Values—The Most Important Criteria

Although competency and talent are important considerations in our selection of candidates, we will only hire people who meet the talent and competency criteria and have the right core values. We strongly believe that to build a lasting company, strong core values are needed as the anchor, which will allow the company to adapt to changes while retaining its core beliefs. In CapitaLand, integrity is a key value that we strictly look for in every employee, as it is the foundation of a socially responsible company. It is made known to all staff, partners and other stakeholders that we have zero tolerance for fraud, bribery and corruption. It is because we have people with integrity that CapitaLand has been successful even in corruption-prone emerging markets.

Active Performance Management

Empowerment—Grow by Letting Go

The Group CEO has about 20 other CEOs of various business units and listed entities reporting to him. His span of control is very broad and wide. How do we make decentralization and delegation work? The answer lies in full empowerment and independence given to business CEOs to lead their business units. Each of the 20 CEOs is delegated the power to hire and fire, power to reward and power on financial authorities. CapitaLand believes that such empowerment is key to leadership development. "Grow by letting go" is one of the philosophies of our leadership development program.

Gaining International Experience

Performance standards at CapitaLand are high, particularly for senior management, and these are consistently applied at all times and at all levels. From the first day CapitaLand was formed, it has operated on the policy of "the best person for the job; the best job for the person." Putting our best people on our biggest opportunities, and not our biggest problems, has been a key tenet of CapitaLand's human resource strategy. For example, we have always made it a point to send only our A-graders to manage and lead our overseas operations and this is an important contributing factor behind CapitaLand's success in expanding overseas.

This philosophy of sending A-graders overseas is adopted from Singapore Airlines.[4] However, besides competency, it is important to note that one should be both bilingual and bicultural in the host country in order to do well overseas. Our experience has taught us that it is not sufficient to be just bilingual.

The performance management process in CapitaLand is rigorous, but not ruthless. Just as we are quick to recognize and reward high performers, we are equally decisive in redeploying or letting go of underperformers. We are decisive about letting underperforming employees go if there is no job fit—we believe this is better for the company and kinder to the underperforming employees in the long term.

Compensation—Pay by Performance

CapitaLand's strong performance-driven culture is reinforced by a robust reward and compensation framework that is closely tied to performance. Our short- and long-term incentive plans are all linked to performance targets. In particular, a substantial portion of senior management's total compensation is tied to stretched performance targets and value creation for shareholders (based on metrics such as Economic Value Added and Wealth Added). There is a deliberate policy of having a sharp differentiation in compensation for high performers.

In addition to cash compensation, CapitaLand's equity-based compensation plans, performance shares and restricted shares plans are awarded to employees to create a stronger sense of ownership of the company and longer-term retention.

Staff Communication and Engagement

To align and engage employees to maximize their contribution, we strongly believe employees need to be in constant communication with their managers and leaders to understand what the company is doing and where it is heading. At the same time, managers need to obtain feedback from their staff on how to improve the company's operations, and hear out suggestions on new ideas and improvements. Regular communication with the staff will also enable managers to identify problems early and see below the tip of the iceberg. Thus, at CapitaLand, we make conscious efforts to create an organization without boundaries and have various initiatives in place to facilitate staff communication and interaction. For example, at the Group as well as SBU level, we have, after the announcement of quarterly financial results, quarterly staff communication sessions (town hall meetings) where the Group or SBU CEO will brief staff on the company's progress, challenges and upcoming initiatives and directions. Every staff should know how the group is doing and where they are heading.

On a more informal but regular basis, our CEOs will make it a point to have meals and interact socially with overseas staff whenever they travel to the overseas offices. All staff are free and in fact encouraged to email their bosses, right up to the Group CEO and Chairman. These are important employee communication channels as they allow the CEOs to be in tune with what is happening on the ground and at the same time provide opportunities for staff to give their feedback personally to senior management.

One unique feature of staff communication at CapitaLand are "Sunday emails" from the Group CEO. This is a regular series of personal Sunday emails from the Group CEO to all staff within the Group. Typically written as anecdotes, these emails help to illustrate and inculcate corporate lessons and values to forge a common corporate culture.

Leadership/Management Training and Development

Upgrading and Further Education

One of the employee value propositions that CapitaLand offers is training and development opportunities that will enable employees to grow and develop their potential. The Group has mapped out a comprehensive development program to match the competency requirements and development needs of all levels of employees. Each and every employee in CapitaLand is given opportunities to upgrade and improve themselves through a variety of in-house training and development programs.

Under the CapitaLand Executive Scholarships program for example, staff can apply for sponsorship for external courses such as Chartered Financial Analyst (CFA) courses, Master of Business Administration (MBA) courses, equivalent postgraduate courses or foreign lan-guage courses.

Corporate Training Institute

In 2006, CapitaLand established its own corporate training institute named "CapitaLand Institute of Management and Business" (CLIMB) to cater to the Group's growing learning and development needs. Besides organizing external courses, CLIMB has also developed a number of in-house leadership and management training programs catered to CapitaLand's specific leadership development needs. Examples of such programs are the CapitaLand Management Program and

CapitaLand Leadership Program, both of which feature the Group CEO as the key speaker. CLIMB has also recently launched the "RE100" training course, which provides 100 hours of customized in-house lessons on real estate fundamentals. The objective of this RE100 program is to provide a quick way of inducting mid-career new hires to key real estate concepts in the areas of land matters, concept planning and design creativity, financing, project management and asset management.

Besides CLIMB, job-specific training courses are also conducted at the Ascott Center for Excellence and the CapitaLand Retail Learning Hub.

Job Rotation

Other than formal training programs, staff development in CapitaLand is also achieved through job rotation and overseas posting. CapitaLand has a policy of allowing staff to request for job rotation after every two years. This policy provides opportunities for staff to work in different business units and/or in different countries, thereby allowing them to explore new interests and challenges and develop new skills.

Localization of Leadership

Real estate is a highly localized business and CapitaLand therefore requires talented local people who understand the local norms of doing business and local consumer requirements. Development of local talents is thus an important aspect of our training and development program. While Singaporeans are usually sent to set up the overseas office operations in the initial years, once these operations are stabilized and we have the right local talents, they will take over the overseas operations. For example, CapitaLand's Thai, Malaysian and Japanese operations are led by a Thai, a Malaysian and a Japanese respectively. In China, the CFO office and the regional offices in Beijing, Hangzhou and Ningbo are all led by local Chinese. This is also an important element for retaining local talents as these local talents would otherwise constantly be on the lookout for opportunities with other companies if they have the mindset that locals will eventually face a glass ceiling.

Company with a Soul

Although CapitaLand is a performance-driven company that focuses on creating value for its shareholders, life at CapitaLand is not all about work. An equally important aspect of human capital management at CapitaLand is providing an environment that takes care of staff welfare and promoting collective giving to community.

Besides offering a comprehensive staff benefits package covering the necessary medical and insurance needs, CapitaLand staff are also entitled to various perks such as staff discounts for purchase of CapitaLand residential units and a yearly family holiday break at Ascott serviced apartments worldwide. To promote work-life balance, CapitaLand staff are also given three days of family event leave per year, on top of their annual leave entitlement.

CapitaLand is committed to be a good corporate citizen and has committed up to 0.5 percent of its annual net profit to CapitaLand Hope Foundation (CHF), its philanthropic arm, to create a better future for underprivileged children. The Foundation focuses only on three main assistance programs: building schools, hospitals or homes for children in need.

The Challenge Ahead: Building a Lasting Company

CapitaLand aims not only to be a prosperous world-class company but also one that lasts. The key to this is to build people with our core values, which will hold the company together through any challenge, and at the same time foster growth and progress. It must take management and leadership succession planning very seriously and carefully. The company will not last if there is no proper succession plan. The Board of Directors reviews the leadership succession plan for its Group CEO and all subsidiary CEOs twice a year. Multiple potential candidates with various suitable succession timeframes are identified. SBU CEOs and younger talents are given opportunities to do presentations to the Board for exposure and to allow the Board to appraise their potential.

Conclusion

Asian companies that are growing into the global arena must have internationally experienced corporate leaders and a strong management bench. However, many Asian companies do not nurture enough CEOs who can lead their companies. They are generally late developers in the area of leadership development. Many have also been hampered because they are family- or state-owned. They are also unable to rely on Asian management talents who had worked in multinational companies operating in Asia, as many of such talents have not been groomed as CEOs.

To address this challenge, rapidly growing and internationalizing Asian companies must provide the right environment to nurture human capital and groom future CEOs. In CapitaLand, our key strategy for building a successful, lasting company is encapsulated in our corporate credo— "Building for people to build people; Building people to build for people."

Through active programs in Attracting Good People, Active Performance Management, Staff Communication and Engagement, and Leadership/Management Training and Development, our human capital strategy focuses on building people with the right skill sets and competencies and right core values in a continuous learning organization and in an organization with a soul. In our view, doing real estate business is not about the commonly known "Timing, Timing, Timing" or "Location, Location, Location." It's about "People, People, People."

Endnotes

1. *Fortune* Global 500, 2008.
2. CapitaLand has ten directors, of which only one is an executive director (President and CEO) while the rest are non-executive directors; four of the latter are foreigners.
3. "The Organizational Challenges of Global Trends: A McKinsey Global Survey," *McKinsey Quarterly*, December 2007.
4. One of CapitaLand's board members, Mr. Lim Chin Beng, used to be the CEO of Singapore Airlines. Mr. Lim had advised CapitaLand to send A-graders overseas. In this way, only the best talents from the company are entrusted to protect and grow the business for the company.

CHAPTER 9

Keeping a Finger on the Pulse

Saw Phaik Hwa

SMRT Corporation Ltd. (SMRT) is a leading multimodal public transport operator and a transport engineering and service solutions provider. Our mission is to be the customer's choice by providing a safe, reliable and friendly travel experience that is enhanced through convenient and innovative services.

Established in 1987 and listed on the Singapore Stock Exchange since 2000, SMRT has a market capitalization of more than S$2.5 billion backed by total assets of S$1.4 billion. Our annual turnover stands at S$879 million for FY2009.

In our core transport business in Singapore, we are committed to offering a safe, reliable and friendly travel experience on our suite of train, bus and taxi services, which are supported by retail amenities and services conveniently located within our stations. Defining our non-fare business are our growing interests in the provision of premium and niche taxi services, leasing of commercial spaces, advertising within our extensive network, operations and maintenance services, project management and engineering consultancy.

Today, SMRT is a market leader recognized for its high standards of corporate governance, corporate transparency and disclosure. At SMRT, our staff is an absolute priority. Through comprehensive retention and development programs, we bring out the best in them so that they can in turn give their best to the company. We also have a long-standing commitment to make a meaningful difference in the lives of those around us, through a sustained program of corporate philanthropy, volunteerism and community outreach. In managing its businesses and driving community initiatives, SMRT's focus is on sustainable development.

Business Leadership in Asia

Generally speaking, Asian companies are still largely either family-driven or personality-based. Company cultures are often shaped by the founder's traditions and values and rise to power is often the right of inheritance versus the best person for the job. At present, there is notable difference between business leadership styles in Asia and America. Culture colors the way things are done, but less so what is done. Asian companies and the national economies, in which they are based, are still evolving and at a different stage of development compared to companies in the West. As Asian companies get more plugged in to global capital markets, they will gravitate towards engaging professional managers who, having gained experience in more established Western corporations, employ leadership styles similar to those used in the West. A more participative style of leadership will become commonplace in Asia and consequently move corporate culture closer to that practiced in Western countries like the United States.

The "professionalization" of Asian companies will change dynamics within and without the organizations as companies increasingly embrace corporate governance and transparency, and move from centralized management control to a more decentralized model of operation. As Asian companies globalize, the need to bring on board seasoned executives with international experience and to employ best practices utilized by established multinational corporations (MNCs) will be inevitable.

Multinational corporations in Asia, on the other hand, have in place varying degrees of control from localization to decentralization. The operation may be headed by a representative from headquarters but senior management is likely to comprise both locals and internationals. While corporate headquarters outside of Asia may provide the key directions, many will have varying degrees of local autonomy, and in some instances allow local considerations to influence decisions made for the city within which the organization operates.

The best of these MNCs do nurture good leaders who understand the need for and practice good governance, and also demonstrate professionalism but may in many ways be limited in terms of total leadership experience as major decisions may still be made by headquarters elsewhere.

Asian Entrepreneurs

There has been a rise of a new generation of entrepreneurs in Asia. These newly minted business leaders are introducing innovations, often challenging current norms and assuming significant personal accountability for inherent risks and outcomes. What they have is the gumption to go beyond the tried and tested in order to seize new business opportunities. However, many may lack the knowledge or skills to manage organizations and put in place good governance as their focus is very much on growing the business.

Leaders for Tomorrow

Whether it is in Asia or beyond, the future requires leaders to not only be adept in their functional roles but who are also deft in the midst of rapid changes as the problems organizations face are constantly evolving and often require immediate attention and decision.

Tomorrow's leaders need to be astute in understanding the complexity of situations and swift in developing solutions that address both current and long-term concerns. There will be greater scrutiny of their leadership, especially as to the sustainability of their business strategies and organizational leadership. The solutions they implement need to be multifaceted as the challenges will be numerous and highly multifarious.

The ideal leader, if there is one, will need to be farsighted, appreciate cultures, possess emotional intelligence, have a global outlook, and be able to seek and maximize opportunities, hence gaining credibility and confidence in the eyes of those they wish to lead.

There will, however, be no "cookie-cutter" style of ideal leadership as business challenges and market situations will be neither straightforward nor certain. Regardless of leadership style, whether autocratic, charismatic or participative, success will be determined more by the ability to adapt swiftly and effectively to varying environmental factors and context. This calls for a leader with clarity of mind and consistency in thought as well as sensitivity to changes in the physical, social and economic environment in order to manage risks and stay ahead of competition and challenges.

Tomorrow's leader will also have to adjust his natural leadership style to match the needs and maturity of his team members. He will need to be attuned to cultural differences. He will need to be firm and yet be able to draw out the best in his team and move them towards a common goal. He will also need to have an eye for identifying talents and grooming future leaders, as thinking of succession only when there is a departure does not bode well for business continuity.

Organizations that address the challenge of leadership succession by looking through the rearview mirror will inevitably get caught when someone steps down or gets removed. The mobility of and competition for talent, fast-paced market changes and growing human capital demands in an expanding business all add to a heightened need to be both strategic and deliberate in succession planning.

Defining the Journey

An indicator of leadership success is the financial viability and business sustainability of the organization. No longer would success be marked purely by short-term results which pay little or no consideration to the long-term health of the company. This means having a clearly defined organizational brand and vision that will set the stage for change and growth forward.

For SMRT Corporation Ltd. (SMRT), the acquisition of TIBS Holdings Ltd. in 2001 added a new dimension to its journey. It meant having to merge two brands and organizational cultures so that the unified organization has one brand, one vision and is guided by a set of common core values. Synergy from the merger came in the form of maximization of resources, lower operating costs and having a choice of talents to put in leadership positions to take the company global.

Successful leaders have the ability to engage and inspire employees to focus on deliverables and business goals. This is critical in a changing world where new challenges and opportunities can either derail or bolster growth plans. Organizations that are ready to capitalize on the opportunities are the ones whose staff live the organizational vision and practice its values when fulfilling their responsibilities. It also has to be a competent team geared for competition.

Another mark of successful leadership is the capacity to satisfy identified stakeholder groups—to anticipate and address their needs. SMRT's experience in this respect has been a colorful one. Transitioning from a train operator to a multimodal transport service provider, a government-owned entity to a public-listed company, our responsibilities have grown manifold in just seven years. Not only are we responsible to the commuters we serve and the more than 6,000 staff as well as some 4,000 taxi partners within our fold, we must also have at heart the interests of shareholders and the community at large. This has taken root in many forms from bringing arts to the heartlands to jointly organized emergency preparedness exercises.

In addition, it is essential that we engage business partners and regulators so that we may broaden our service offerings beyond transportation. This is evidenced by the expansion of our retail and media offerings.

The mindset change and progress we have seen over the years are due largely to our conscious efforts to educate and empower our staff. We ground them from the start, challenging them to be flexible and holistic in solving problems, especially when expanding our business interests, such as our taxi or chartering services, or when taking the business abroad. From controlling costs to increasing revenue, these have all been possible because the team is commercially and financially astute and everyone understands the business needs and goals.

Beyond traditional bottom-line markers, the success of forward-looking leadership will be characterized by the genuine commitment to the greater community and to the environment. Business ethics and organizational propriety will have to stretch beyond corporate governance and transparency, and embrace responsibility for business impact on all stakeholders and the environment.

In keeping with our commitment to be an industry leader in environmental stewardship, we are focusing our efforts on cultivating green values and encouraging behavioral change in employees and commuters through multiple platforms. Since we started operations, there has been no let up in our efforts to drive both environmental conservation and sustainable development.

To continue on this path of economic growth and development means we must have the leadership capital to sustain the organization and at the same time, a living plan that allows us to draw out the best in our people.

At SMRT, leadership succession is planned as a subset of our entire suite of talent development and talent management efforts. It is executed in line with the organization's current and future business goals, and aimed at building leadership strength, and systematically closing the gap between human capital needs the organization has, and leadership and talent demands the organization will face in order to respond effectively to future business challenges.

SMRT's HR Solution

We believe in the value of investing in human capital, as honing a constant talent core ensures a steady stream of leaders who are ready to take the helm. Our Talent Management Framework, anchored on three programs—Devel@p, Nurture and ACE—has been progressively implemented for the various pools of talents within SMRT (see Figure 9.1).

FIGURE 9-1. SMRT TALENT MANAGEMENT FRAMEWORK

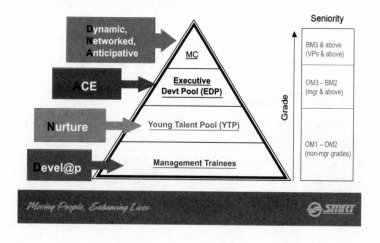

Devel@p

Targeted at bringing in SMRT's entry talent and leadership pipeline, Devel@p (also known as **De**veloping **E**xecutives into **L**eaders **A**ccelerated **P**rogram) is an intensive **one-year accelerated program** that equips our Management Trainees with foundational understanding of SMRT's core business and shapes their attitude and aptitude necessary for assuming management executive positions with SMRT. The program aims to develop talents into Business Management Grade (BM and above) executives by the time they turn 35.

In June 2008, we welcomed our inaugural intake of 23 management trainees under Devel@p. Following a one-week customized induction to the corporation, the management trainees were placed on a 15-month program to equip them with the foundational understanding of SMRT's core business and prepare them to assume key executive management positions in SMRT.

Nurture

Nurture, as the name of the program suggests, seeks to uncover, grow and cultivate promising young talents who are nonmanagers below 30 years old to their fullest potential. The company does this by creating opportunities for these promising individuals to assume responsibilities in various corporate projects so as to help them gain greater confidence. The pool of young talents under this program is SMRT's secondary talent and leadership pipeline. Since the start of this program in 2008, four of the 15 young talents in this pool have been promoted to managers with expanded portfolios.

ACE

Deeper into the rungs of talents at Managerial and above grades, between 31 and 40 years old, the Executive Development Pool undertakes the ACE program to equip them with the business Acumen, Competence and Cutting Edge to be business leaders of tomorrow. Of the 30 talents in this pool, 17 have been promoted to vice presidents, directors and heads of departments, and are driving businesses both locally and overseas.

Proactive Future Planning

Defining the business would require the full understanding of planned business directions and mapping the vision to the current and future competencies required to achieve the objectives at each level. This is in addition to identifying the existing and future roles these competencies would relate to.

In arriving at the critical competencies, SMRT then assesses the current strength of our leaders and talents, complete with the backdrop of an analysis of the gaps between the requirements of the future roles and where the employees are currently placed. In the process, specific Individual Development Plans would be developed to enable the talent pipeline to prepare adequately for their future roles.

In a recent reorganization of one of the departments, we made a conscious decision to reassign long-serving senior staff to advisory roles so as to give younger talents the opportunity to assume leadership roles in the department. With the support of senior advisors and a hands-on, conducive and supportive environment, the young talents should thrive and make good progress in their new role.

The SMRT Leader

To ensure SMRT remains relevant and competitive in the next lap, a set of leadership competencies, the **SMRT Leader Competencies,** necessary for our sustained success, excellent leadership skills and high performance culture were developed by SMRT's senior management team (see Figure 9.2). The SMRT Leader comprises 23 behavioral competencies relating to vital areas such as thinking, leading, emotional and managing aspects. These competencies are central to the development of leaders with clarity of vision and thought, and who possess the ability to engage, motivate and build trust as they continue to grow the company, keeping in mind SMRT's commitment to sustainable development.

This model was communicated to staff via platforms such as the "Annual Leadership Convention," "Tea for Your

FIGURE 9-2. THE **SMRT** LEADER COMPETENCIES

The SMRT Leader - *Six Facets*

Mind-view
looks at the capacity of a positive mind to think strategically and holistically, allowing the individual to prioritize tasks and make good decisions.

Heart-ware
looks at the ability of the individual to regulate his/her emotions and exercises management courage, in the context of a positive organizational vision.

People Management
looks at how the individual builds an effective team through leading by example, inspiration, coaching, empowerment and recognition, on the basis of effective communication.

Relationship Management
looks at the way an individual effectively interacts with his/her peers and other levels above, by being a team player.

Resource Management
looks at the ability of an individual to optimize the usage of resources through planning, organizing, and being a creative and innovative change agent.

Values
encompasses our SMRT core values which includes Excellence, Integrity, and being Committed and Dependable.

Moving People, Enhancing Lives ⊜ SMRT

■ *179* ■

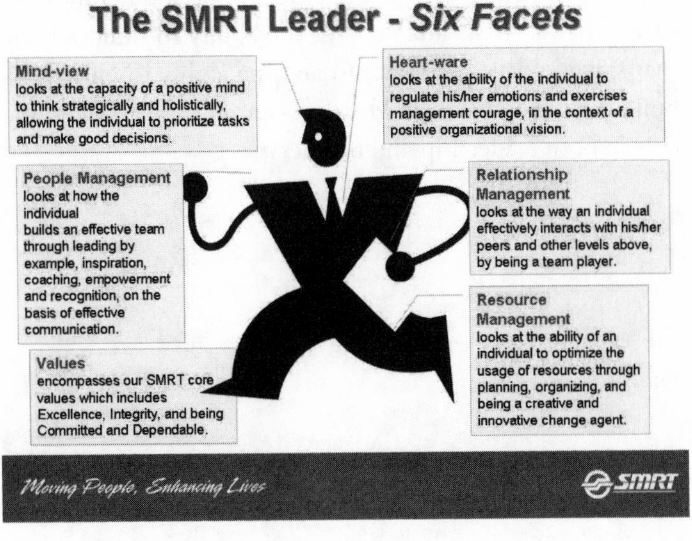

Thoughts" and "SMRT Leaders Training and Exchange." To help develop and reinforce these behaviors, a 360-degree Feedback was rolled out to all Managers and above. This process included self-awareness, action planning, executive coaching (for the management committee) and IMPACT coaching (for all department heads). In addition, all business units have established in their Divisional Functional Action Plans that they will apply the SMRT Leader Model in their daily operations.

Tomorrow's Leader

No business leader or organization thrives by assuming that the same old ways of leading and doing business will continue to work in every situation or in the future. A successful leader, like a successful organization, must continually be sensitive to shifts in the situational context and be astute enough to correctly determine the interventions that are required to sustain growth and attain desired outcomes. Situational awareness, adaptability, the ability to build a brand that stakeholders can relate to and the ability to engage and build the trust of stakeholders are central to sustainable success in both leadership and business.

CHAPTER 10

Leadership Challenges in the Transformation of Healthcare

Liak Teng Lit

In the initial years after a major restructuring exercise in 2000, the challenge at Alexandra Hospital was to turn around the organization by getting the fundamentals right and putting the patient at the center of all that we do. By aligning the organization and putting discipline around the right processes, the leadership team was able to achieve a successful transformation.

The next challenge for Alexandra will be much bigger. It will involve not only managing a new hospital but also transforming the model of healthcare. There is no set precedent. Alexandra's leadership team cannot simply repeat successful solutions of the past in addressing new challenges. It will need to chart new paths where none currently exists. Different leadership competencies will be needed. Efforts will have to be placed on identifying the next level of talents. And most importantly, innovation will have to be the next mantra.

Transformation of Alexandra Hospital 1.0

Alexandra Hospital is a 350-bed hospital located in the southern part of Singapore. It was the last public hospital to be restructured in 2000. Prior to restructuring, the hospital had suffered from poor public perception, low demand and negative financial performance.

The journey to transform the hospital itself was not easy. It took patience, determination and courage. But the tenacity paid off and the performance of the hospital began to turn around. Alexandra Hospital has topped the Ministry of Health patient satisfaction surveys for the past five years, received numerous awards and returned to financial health. The hospital today is generally well-regarded for its innovation in delivering high-quality patient care and services and is often cited for its care for the environment.

In 2008, the hospital was incorporated as a separate corporate entity known as Alexandra Health Private Limited (AHPL). Most of the board of directors were drawn from the private sector. The mandate from the Minister for Health was for AHPL to innovate and transform healthcare.

Existing Leadership Team

The majority of the current leadership team was assembled in 2000. Key leaders were drawn from different public and private hospitals. The team was intentionally diverse in background, education and even personalities. Our philosophy was that if two of us thought alike, then one of us was redundant. The diversity was important as we had numerous challenges to solve that required different perspectives. Team members, however, were united through the sharing of common core values and the central philosophy of putting the patient first in everything that we do.

The second-tier leadership consisting of heads of departments were drawn partly from within the organization and some were hired from other institutions. Leadership selection was based mainly on seniority in their respective professional areas. Few had formal or even informal management and leadership training prior to their appointments.

The supervisors and executives on the ground today are a mix of professional and non-professional staff. Leadership and management training for this group varied widely. Some had formal training while others had gone through short training programs organized by the hospital or by external providers.

The practitioners, doctors, nurses, therapists and other healthcare staff are drawn from various universities and polytechnics here and overseas. Their philosophies and paradigms are mainly influenced and shaped by their professional affiliations and the institutions where they were trained.

Aligning Diversity Through Management Leadership Training and Development

The diversity of talents was crucial and critical in helping to bring the hospital back on its feet as there was an urgent need to change practices within the hospital. New systems and processes had to be introduced. The best leaders for this type of transformation were the system thinkers and decisive, fast movers.

On the other hand, change in management involved much emotion. People who had been in the organization for years were anxious and unhappy when changes were introduced. Managing emotions and addressing personal concerns required leaders who were empathetic and sensitive.

But for an organization to change successfully, it is imperative for everyone to row in the same direction. The diversity of leaders presented its own set of challenges. Different personalities have different perspectives and the organization could easily be paralyzed by differences of opinions and conflicts. It was important, therefore, to align the leaders and their teams around shared objectives and create a common language to facilitate constructive debate.

First, great attempts were made to hire the right people. Potential recruits were put through multiple interviews by key leaders. The people hired had to display the key 4Es personality traits (Energy, Energize, Edge, Execution) coupled with Passion and Authenticity.

But that was not enough. People had to share a similar vision and we implemented a training and development framework to unite the organization.

New employees are initiated into the organization over a two-day orientation program. Learning from the Ritz-Carlton hotel, the orientation program is conducted by the top leadership team personally and not simply by the human resources department. New hires are systematically inducted to the organizational values, philosophy, strategy and approaches through a mix of programs.

Supervisors and managers are given a list of books that they are strongly encouraged to read. These include *The 7 Habits of Highly Effective People* by Stephen Covey, *Built to Last* and *Good to Great* by James Collins, *Winning* by Jack Welch, *Heroic Leadership* by Chris Lowney, *The Toyota Way* by Jeffrey Liker, *The Innovator's Prescription* by Clayton Christensen, among others. The books serve to create a common understanding and use of common language for the team.

Book reviews are held weekly during the lunch hour to promote a reading culture and to encourage teams to share their knowledge. It is also a rapid way for continued learning to permeate through the organization.

Numerous in-house training programs including Service Quality, Quality Improvement, understanding Toyota Production Systems and professional and technical trainings are also used to develop a process and quality mindset at all levels of the organization. Staff also have a chance to share their quality improvement success stories, big or small, during vision alignment sessions and administrative meetings.

Staff who aspire to take on administrative and leadership roles are encouraged to sign up for MBAs and other relevant programs on a part-time basis. Promising individuals are sponsored partly or fully for their courses. Many mid-level staff signed on for MBA and other postgraduate management programs to upgrade themselves at their own cost. A few of the high potential staff were fully or partially sponsored by the hospital.

Learning by Doing

Training is only one aspect of promoting a "learning organization." The best learning often takes place when staff have a chance to apply what they learn.

The hospital promotes a "Just-Do-It" culture. Staff at all levels are encouraged to take ownership and do what is necessary to solve problems. "Do first. Seek forgiveness if necessary" is an often repeated and celebrated statement in the organization.

Staff are often challenged to take on roles beyond their fields of training and experience to stretch and widen their perspectives. Promising staff are encouraged to take on leadership roles in quality improvement initiatives and project management of major events, including Quality Circles, Six Sigma, launch of new services, as well as hospital functions such as Dinner and Dance, Nurses' Day and Quality Convention.

The most challenging assignments are given to the most promising staff. Typically, a young leader is identified and approached by their manager to take on an assignment. Staff are also encouraged to step forward to take on assignments in which they have interest.

A cross-functional, complementary team of five to six are then assembled to work on the assignment. One or more senior staff members will mentor and help the team to set clear objectives, benchmarks, measurements, deadlines and to articulate a vision of success for the project.

Their performances in these activities are closely monitored with the aim of helping the team members grow and develop. Promising high-potential individuals are regularly invited to the hospital's senior management meetings for exposure.

For all key initiatives and events, the teams are required to present After-Action-Review with senior management. The objective is to ensure learning at personal and organizational levels at every opportunity.

Unexpected crises have also presented great opportunity for leadership development over the years. The SARS outbreak in 2003, the tsunami in 2004 and other minor internal situations had allowed those with leadership qualities to rise to the occasion and shine. Our timely establishment of defensive protocol, system and processes during the SARS outbreak enabled the hospital to stay SARS-free even while we increased our capacity to take in patients from other public hospitals.

In the aftermath of the tsunami, a team of volunteers from the hospital was among the first to reach Aceh to offer assistance. Each of these crisis situations has surfaced effective leaders who were subsequently assigned higher responsibility in the hospital.

Another key learning opportunity actually comes from listening to the patients. Focus group meetings are organized with patients every month to get their direct inputs and around 30 to 40 staff ranging from nurses and administrators to chefs and porters attend these sessions to listen to feedback and work on improvements. The ultimate test of whether the hospital is doing the right things is at the point of patient contact. These sessions help to keep the organization sane and real.

Each year the hospital participates in a few key professional conferences overseas. The hospital also organizes a few mission-specific study visits overseas. Teams of about ten to 15 individuals are carefully selected for these five- to seven-day trips. Usually led by the CEO and/or Chairman Medical Board, these extended trips also serve as an opportunity for individual and group learning. Team members are asked to share their learning and to implement what they learn upon their return.

Staff are also strongly encouraged to be involved with volunteer work outside the organization, preferably in leadership roles. This not only furthers the objective of doing good and contributing back to the community; it also helps staff to widen their experiences and perspectives.

Transformation 2.0: The Next Five Years

Like most hospitals, much of the focus of AH is on treating patients with acute illnesses. Overspecialization and subspecialization can cause medical care to be episodic and compartmentalized. Patients are often sent from pillar to posts. Current care model can be best described as "episodic, compartmentalized illness care of body parts" (see Figure 10.1). Not enough is being done to help individuals uncover hidden problems before they fall ill, and to anticipate and address medical problems of old age.

FIGURE 10-1. EPISODIC COMPARTMENTALIZED ILLNESS CARE MODEL

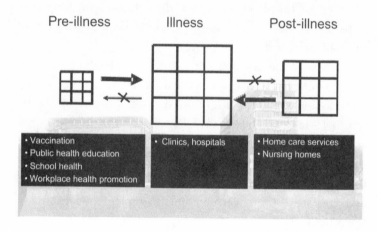

The Minister of Health has challenged the team to question all established assumptions relating to healthcare, and to innovate and experiment with the aim of trans-forming the industry.

The team has conceptualized a new model of care that places much greater emphasis on health (see Figure 10.2). Best described as "head-to-toe, lifelong anticipatory healthcare of the whole person," the new model requires a fundamental re-examination of almost all the roles and functions in healthcare.

FIGURE 10-2. HEAD-TO-TOE LIFELONG ANTICIPATORY HEALTHCARE OF THE WHOLE PERSON MODEL

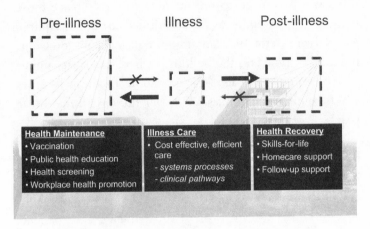

From transforming a hospital in the earlier days, the team is now tasked to transform the much bigger issue of healthcare. There is no established new model of care that the organization can copy. Doing more of the same is not a viable option. The team needs to chart new paths where none currently exists. The organization will be undergoing a major expansion in capacity and capability over the next three to five years.

In 2010, the team will move to a brand new hospital built in the Northern part of the island. The new Khoo Teck Puat Hospital (KTPH) is situated in the heartlands of Yishun. For the new hospital, the Minister of Health has challenged the team to "build a hospital designed with patients unambiguously at the center of the focus, with technology fully exploited for the benefit and convenience of patients . . . It will be a hospital which is well linked . . . and to which the patients can be transferred seamlessly . . . It is to be a hassle-free hospital."

The move from the existing 350-bed Alexandra Hospital into a larger 550-bed at KTPH in 2010 means that there will be a need to recruit new staff to replace those who leave, as well as to fill additional positions required for a larger operation. Planning for a new generation Community Hospital and the building of new specialists ambulatory centers have also started. Some of these facilities will be built and commissioned over the next three to five years.

The intention is to remodel care in the various facili-ties by segmenting patients based on different needs. Each facility will then focus on delivering specialized care effectively and efficiently.

The KTPH will focus on "Fast Medicine," i.e., patients with acute, urgent and critical needs. The aim is to diagnose and treat these patients efficiently, effectively and quickly.

The Community Hospital will focus on "Slow Medicine," providing a full range of services for older patients, from wellness and health promotion programs for the elderly, to geriatric assessment, treatment and management for those with multiple medical conditions, and end-of-life care for the dying.

Part of KTPH and the ambulatory centers will provide "Cruise Medicine," delivering highly efficient health screening for the masses and chronic diseases management programs for those with diabetes and other chronic diseases.

Together, these entities will work with other partners, including General Practitioners (GPs), Polyclinics and nursing homes to provide a spectrum of services from wellness programs to chronic disease management, and from acute care interventions to palliative and end-of-life care.

Apart from emphasizing head-to-toe healthcare, the new model must also address the other huge phenomenon of rising healthcare costs and rising expectations as Singapore takes on first-world status as a country. A huge part of healthcare cost is related to manpower cost which is steadily rising. Technology will be key to the transformation of healthcare, but this also comes with a hefty price tag.

Innovation will be a key success factor. Innovation is not just about buying better equipment. It is about shifting thinking outside of current boundaries to bring about imaginative and dramatically different solutions. Process innovations are needed to reduce waiting time and increase patient contact time, and to reduce unnecessary activity and increase productivity. People innovation is needed to bring about a new breed of leaders and on the ground, to reduce errors and increase service levels.

This new paradigm is also a model that requires close partnerships to enable seamless care.

The New Leadership Paradigm

The current leadership team has performed adequately for the past and present. However, the organization has probably reached the top of the first S-curve. The hospital has successfully moved from a low-image hospital to one with a standard of healthcare that matched, and in some areas, exceeded current industry practice.

The next phase is about exceeding the best benchmarks in other industries. For example, the hospital aims to match or exceed Singapore Airlines and Ritz-Carlton who are far ahead of the healthcare industry in terms of service quality. The next curve is also about transforming the model of care from the currently hospital-centric, involving the treatment of body parts, to one that is patient-centric, involving vertically integrated care of the whole person.

This transformation is very different from the creation of a new and improved version of an existing hospital. Diversity, patience, determination and courage steered us out of muddy waters into a clear lake surrounded by natural landscape. The focus was in aligning the team, putting discipline around the right processes so that we can do things faster, cheaper, better and safer for patients. All these will continue to be important, but the next course is to steer the ship into uncharted waters where maps and compasses, while helpful, are not adequate.

We will need to step up and re-craft existing leadership competencies. We need a more focused approach in identifying the next level of talents. Most importantly, as mentioned earlier, innovation will need to be our next mantra.

Re-crafting Leadership Competencies

The qualities of leadership that was good enough for the past and present may not be good enough for the future. Leadership competencies of the existing team will need to be brought to the next plane. If we led with 80 percent perspiration and 20 percent inspiration, the reverse is probably now true. We need closer to 80 percent inspiration while the other 20 percent continues to build upon the tested processes and discipline of the past several years.

There is a greater need for leaders who are comfortable with ambiguity and uncertainty. There is also a need for leaders to paint a compelling vision of the future, and to explain goals and objectives in clear and simple terms and set the right priorities. We also need leaders who can see around the corner; people who are able to think of solutions, not just for the here and now, but taking into consideration possible future trends and directions. They must then have the courage of conviction to lead the way onto the uncharted path.

Many healthcare professionals are deep specialists in their fields. They learn and interact closely with their peers outside of the organization and their perspectives are shaped by their professional cohort rather than within the hospital. With their professional knowledge and paradigm, they often find it hard to see things differently, from the holistic hospital context. The skills used in the diagnosis and treatment of patient issues are different from those required to lead an organization forward. Helping our professional staff see things differently and to unlearn is a key leadership challenge.

The adage that supervisors hire and promote in their own image is probably partially true. While some senior leaders are able to recognize and develop talent, others are less effective. As a healthcare organization, the hospital probably has too many caring individuals in leadership positions. While empathy and caring are good qualities for healthcare, an "over balance" of this attribute sometimes results in leaders settling for mediocrity for fear of hurting others' feelings.

While some leaders are more demanding and challenge juniors to stretch and thus help them grow, others are too forgiving and fail to help their subordinates rise in their thinking and performance. Fundamentally, there is no consensus at the senior level on the balance beween "love" and "tough love" within the organization. As the Chairman Medical Board pointed out correctly, the balance is situational. However, with the greater challenge and complexity ahead, there is a need to shift the balance towards a demand for a higher level of performance.

Fundamentally, we need talent to recognize and develop talent. Not all key position holders have the talent themselves to meet the challenges ahead.

Identifying the Next Level of Talents

There is an immediate need to step up the recruitment to increase staff strength from 1,700 to approximately 3,000 over the next five years. Much of the people growth will consist of "new blood" from outside, including from other industries, to bring in fresh ideas, perspectives and competencies. The preference is to insert new hires at third to fourth levels in the organization, immerse them in the culture and build linkages. This will allow them to grow and give them time to prove themselves before assuming higher positions.

Competent mid-level staff are given challenging assignments with the goal of accelerating their development for higher leadership positions. Already, some are showing promise and rising to the challenge.

A more formal and structured talent management program has been organized with input from the Board and the board subcommittee. The senior team is working on a clearer definition of desired leadership qualities to ensure greater consistency in hiring, training, development and deployment. This team of approximately five senior leaders will be the talent spotters and will track and groom new talents over time.

Rapid advancement in medical sciences and technology will pose new challenges. Healthcare employees of the future need to be highly trained and competent, and yet have the humility to constantly learn, unlearn and relearn.

Digitization and automation of information to facilitate seamless care as well as advances in tele-medicine to reduce waiting time and unnecessary travel will become increasingly important. Healthcare workers must, therefore, become more comfortable and proficient in the use of technology.

Patients are also becoming better educated and the Internet has provided them with greater access to information and research that used to be available only to practitioners and doctors. Patients who are better informed are demanding to be involved in their own care.

The prescriptive nature of healthcare has to give way to a more collaborative model where practitioners and patients work together to decide the most appropriate treatment. Healthcare workers must, therefore, work with an open heart and open mind. They also need better communication skills so that collaborative rather than instructive consultation can take place.

More structured and formal in-house supervisory and management training programs are being designed and will be rolled out later this year. External experts have been invited to contribute to the design of these programs. A large part of the training will be delivered by leaders in the organization using actual stories of past experience to illustrate values, philosophies and approaches.

The performance appraisal system has been redesigned to match and encourage the right behaviors and practices. The ability and willingness to coach and mentor future leaders are key requirements for all supervisory and management positions.

The goal is to put in place the top 30 to 40 core leaders and another 300 to 400 in the third to fourth levels in the organization within five years. At the core, the key leaders will need to be highly competent, respected individuals who are walking logos of the organizational values and philosophy. They in turn will select, develop and nurture future leaders required to build a great institution.

Innovation: Our Next Mantra

Innovation is critical in moving the organization into the next S-curve. It is important for the leadership to encourage, enable and protect innovation that can shift the paradigm. It is much easier to continue making incremental improvements to what we are currently doing and feel that it is good enough. Innovation and change can be risky and to be out there doing things differently from others can be very uncomfortable.

Leadership has to recognize this and make concerted efforts to provide the right environment and encouragement to nurture new ideas. The competencies required of the leader include the ability to recognize ideas and encourage risk taking, even if the ideas are controversial and have not been done before. Then they must have the courage to support their staff and provide resources needed for experimentation. They must also learn how to accept failure as part of the learning process and in so doing, protect those who dare to innovate and question.

It also calls for letting things go—processes and standards that perhaps we had perfected and thus built a strong bonding or pride may no longer be relevant. At the very least, we need to experiment with new ways of doing things in parallel. It is the digital camera versus the analog camera phenomenon. Healthcare, for example, would have to increasingly embrace the digital world and use it to its advantage, such as in experimenting with tele-medicine. It cannot replace the personal touch of the physician, but it can be leveraged and incorporated into the existing model to address urgent care issues and reduce travel and waiting time.

Conclusion

In the first few years, the challenge at Alexandra Health was to turn the hospital around by focusing on getting the fundamentals right and putting the patient at the center of all that we do. The leadership assembled at that point was appropriate for the task and was able to deliver this successfully.

The next phase involves not only managing a new hospital, but transforming the model of healthcare. There is no set precedent and this requires a different level of leadership. The team cannot simply rely on repeating successful solutions of the past to address new challenges. A good foundation has been laid, but now the team has to go beyond that to raise the bar on thinking and performance.

It is easy to say it, but embracing new ways of doing things and thinking outside of the current paradigm is hard work. It takes vision and commitment. There is a lot left to do.

CHAPTER 11

How Good Can We Be?

Fergus Balfour[1]

The title is chosen to reflect the need for even the best organizations to remain in a constant state of renewal. They are not constrained by targets but powered by zeal to exceed their own expectations. All employees gain energy and confidence from looking at how high they have already climbed and then use this to scale the next summit. They may stumble and fall but they have the capacity for fast recovery. In essence, they practice the "do-fail-learn-do cycle."

Overview of the Business

Unilever is a 40 billion Euro business which has 180,000 employees. Over 50 percent of its turnover is in Foods. Almost 40 percent of this turnover is in Asia, Africa and Eastern Europe. Within Unilever, UFS (Unilever Foodsolutions) competes in the OOH (Out of Home) segment of the market. The market size of OOH is estimated to be about 22 billion Euros. Unilever has a significant share of it.

The Market Environment

Eating in OOH operates at all levels of income; from the basic hole-in-the-wall eateries/LET all the way up to fine dining as seen in Figure 11.1.

FIGURE 11-1

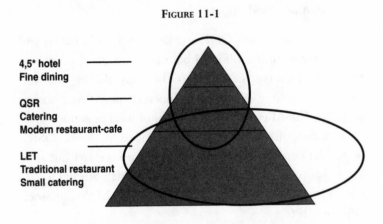

4,5* hotel
Fine dining

QSR
Catering
Modern restaurant-cafe

LET
Traditional restaurant
Small catering

Since 2009, the market has moved from low double-digit growth to zero or negative growth. However, five trends which were established since the year 2000 are deeply embedded and will restore and drive growth to previous levels. They are, namely:

1. Out-of-home consumption continues to grow. More will be spent each year driven by population growth and rising income and an ever increasing demand for better quality.
2. Food and labor costs grow driven by shortage.

3. Shortage of skilled "chefs"—potential employees attracted by other jobs.
4. Need for more consistency and hygiene standards driven by government health and food safety regulations as seen in, for example, Singapore and Australia and increasingly in China.
5. Scratch conversion as convenience products save time and cost and allow chefs to spend time on quality, which will allow them to charge more and differentiate their food outlets.

Competition in the OOH market is highly diversified and as yet remains unconsolidated both in terms of suppliers and providers. In terms of suppliers there are the big international players (e.g., Nestlé and Unilever), major Asia players (e.g., Lee Kum Kee) and then a mass of local operators.

In terms of providers, Quick Service Operators (QSR), (e.g., McDonald's and KFC) have grown very fast but now local chains are the biggest engine of growth attracting talent and providing a big opportunity for Initial Public Stock Offering (IPO).

Business Issues in Asia, Africa and Middle East

Unilever Foodsolutions (UFS) is a major player in the market whose product range is seen as premium. We do not just sell products but seek to find solutions which support operators in three ways:

1. Help them achieve greater profitability
2. Help them achieve better quality

3. Help them achieve greater differentiation

This approach, coupled with increased focus on Channel Marketing skills and using our Sales Tools to focus on key customers, has given us very strong growth in the last five years in this region. The key market issue in 2009 is growth. Markets are either flat or negative. Consumers still eat out as a way of life but seek to reduce their cost. Operators look to suppliers to reduce their costs. In this environment of zero to negative growth, we need to ensure we are the provider which remains most relevant to our customers. The strategy remains correct because quality, profitability and differentiation are at the heart of running food outlets successfully and at all price levels. However, our environment has drastically changed.

As one Japanese leader commented: "It's not the strongest species that survive, nor the most intelligent, but the ones most responsive to change."

So the big issues to work on are how to ensure that our **leadership** can help our **organization** adapt to the new environment, continue to attract the right **talent** and then combining these three levers, drive growth above the market average. The game changing opportunity is for UFS to emerge from this recession with stronger market share and consolidate a leadership position for the time when the market returns to strong growth.

What we need to do is probably best summarized by Vice-Admiral Nelson in his eve of battle speech before the Battle of Trafalgar at the beginning of the nineteenth century: "To show patience in adversity, vision beyond the end of one's nose, a steady nerve, resolution when disappointed, and a belief in the way one's organization is going."

Some Best Practices

The next section on best practices will explain our approach under three headings:

1. Attracting the right talent
2. How to make an organization adaptive and responsive to change
3. How to imbue the right philosophy and practice of leadership

Through this we can answer the title question of this paper which is, "How good can we be?" This is the question which only the best organizations ask themselves and have the capability to answer. Inevitably, these headings interweave with each other but separating them is helpful for clarity.

Attracting the Right Talent

Our business in this region of Asia, Africa and the Middle East is spread out over 20 countries and they comprise one of the most culturally diverse regions on the planet. Fortunately, they all eat out but their food tastes differ and in any case food trends are fusing and adapting to each other. The East is influencing the West (the chili trend) and the West is influencing the East (sauces—e.g., prawns in carbonara sauce as served in Hong Kong).

We need to find talent which respects the difference but approaches the market with a common philosophy. But like Singapore Airlines, we need to understand that we are only as good as the people who are at the frontline of our business. They have direct contact with hotel restaurants and catering outlets. Their quality, confidence, ability to cope with setbacks and face situations we cannot predict will define our organization. We have a substantial number of these sales consultants worldwide whom we directly manage and many are in this region. We have many more who work for our distributors. It is as if we are one of the largest food training universities in the world. We also have shareholders who expect us to win in the market and make consistent and ever-increasing profits. You can only do that with a high growth mindset.

This high growth mindset is the first and one of the most important practices to impart to our talents and directly influence how we organize and lead. It is hard to sustain throughout the year. A good way to test ourselves, and I know we fall short of this, is to borrow from the Silicon Valley culture, which can be summarized as follows:

> *Firstly it's clear that start-ups remain a highly attractive option despite the crash of tech stocks. Their promise fits the mindset of the younger generation which expects three things: a high level of autonomy, a sense of ownership and the potential for the individual to make a visible impact.*

If you combine people who want to make an impact in the market with very tough growth targets, you build the ability to constantly improve. The difficult task is how to do this such that the targets are energizing but not threatening. That comes from building capability but also a constant hunger to improve.

Our frontline people are in the marketplace often by themselves. We want them to feel they can make the impact. This requires a high level of training and confi-dence. We have through time learned the common sales skills that we need to test for. Some key attributes stand out; the most obvious is a fascination and interest in eating and enjoying food. But just as important is the capability of seeking and securing information from our customers.

The frontline is dependent on a strong supporting structure. But often it feels they serve those back in the office. As one person said about an organization:

From root to crown, ideas flow up and orders down

But that will ultimately sound the death knell of the organization because, as Singapore Airlines has successfully shown, keeping the frontline sharp is a tough long-term task. The key is to bring the customer into the everyday business of our offices.

It is essential if we are to have a chance to answer "How good can we be?" This is because that is much more defined by the market facing part of the organization.

A good question for each person to ask, particularly leaders at all levels, is:

- Does this work need doing?
- Does it lead to growth?
- Do I need to do it or can it be delegated?

We must also recognize that our experience as a market leader means that we recruit people and train them and then in many cases they are highly employable. It is the perpetual cycle of inexperience. Of course we will keep key resources but we will need to face the fact that we will be in a perpetual training cycle *and* the demand for quality is always rising.

Other practices which I have learned in recent learning circles are:

- Referral hiring—our good people know good people so we can reward them for recruitment and helping to improve the quality of our organization.
- Recruit against capabilities defined by our customers. This way you remain current and relevant. You will also improve diversity as you infuse the organization with new blood but who will by definition be different because they are up to date. In particular look for learning agility.
- Ensure the feedback conversations to employees include tough messages but also make sure that this is set in a context where personal connections are built with individuals and the assessment is done by a mix of people and not just one person.
- Target the people you want to find more carefully. Look to see that their values are aligned but ensure there is a good understanding of what you are going to demand for the price (reward) they will get. In essence, be more differentiated.
- On focusing on strengths versus weaknesses—a lovely anecdote: do not try to teach a pig to sing—it wastes your time and annoys the pig.

How to Make an Organization Adaptive and Responsive to Change

A good place to start is to make sure the organization is absolutely honest with where it stands—what I call organizational integrity. Many years ago I made the mistake of fooling myself on how good we were (note—not how good we can be). My boss then made it clear that I should *publicly* apologize to the whole of my team (it was large) that I had let them down by not facing the truth and that if ever I did it again he would personally ensure I was fired. But it taught me a valuable lesson in facing the truth.

Facing the truth is one thing but how do you teach recovery ability and why is this important? The harder organizations push, the more likely they will fall over. In one of our businesses, the staff was faced with difficult issues on product quality. They had to face the fact that if they did not change almost the complete range, then their business would stop. But they refused to allow the team to use this as an excuse to miss their target. In the end, they did both and taught themselves an important lesson in recovery.

An organization can be brutally honest with itself and it can build recovery capability but it rarely succeeds without speed. How do you do this and retain the benefits of size? Size and speed are difficult to combine.

As the chairman of BMW said: "The big do not always beat the small but the fast always beat the slow."

So how do you get a large organization to be fast? We used to be very fast because each country ran its own operation. But then we found that there was much duplication of activities and not enough leverage of best practices, so we need to try other ways to organize ourselves.

Many of our ways of working in an organization are based on what I call an ownership model (what is usually called a contract of employment). But going into the future, the engagement model might be more of who works *with* us, not *for* us. You see Apple employing this to try to get developers who do not work for Apple to do this for their iPhone in order to secure its clients. One external test of organizational health is this: Do people want to work with you because you are exciting and vibrant?

How to Imbue the Right Philosophy and Practice of Leadership

A good way to look at this is: Do we give people the freedom to be creative, a chance to bring out the best in people where what they do matters and is this then rewarded in the pocket book and the soul? I have always felt that this is what leadership was all about because this is what great leaders can do. But it is hard and in particular it is important for leaders to understand the difference between doing content (which we easily gravitate to) and setting context; these are the true tasks of a leader. Why is context setting so important?

Leadership can make a difference to context in three ways:

(a) Energy
(b) Targets Value/Environment
(c) How teams work

The reason is that these three are at the heart of the engagement model. The engagement model is the key to long-term sustainable growth. It provides the fuel for continuous improvement and the constant will to ask, "How good can we be?"

Energy

Leadership should focus activities and people on valuing growth. Making this happen requires energy, and the collective energy of the organization is our most precious asset. So the questions to ask are whether managers create or drain energy. Ask the same regarding activities and whether they help the business grow. Do our people feel that what they spend time on is where their passion is engaged and where they feel they do their best work?

A good test is to question whether people feel they have more energy at the end of the day. This energy comes from the people they work for or the work they do or both. If it is not there it may be because the people they work for are not inspiring or the work they do lacks meaning.

From personal experience, when I feel a lack of energy, I go out to the market. It always works.

One of our businesses was faced with an extreme threat in a key category. They had been losing volume to a low-price competitor and you could feel the energy flowing out of the business. But its leader demanded that the whole company, regardless of function, went to the market for a week to see what was going on and find out what they could do about it. The result—recharged energy, the problem was clear to all and the solution was found. The business is now growing.

When you show a person how the tool can help them make a difference and impact, the energy level goes up and this is "contagious."

Targets Value/Environment

Again leadership makes the difference. How?

Leadership does not focus on solving problems but tries to create an environment where great talent can perform. They will test this by seeing if their people feel it is worthy of their commitment.

But this does not mean easy targets. On the contrary, it gives clarity but then creates tough targets which stretch people in their jobs. Leaders are very clear about what they want people to achieve. They spend time on coaching them on ways these goals can be achieved but without getting in the way or taking over. They let go. But good leadership never fails to manage difficult people issues.

Good leadership focuses on creating events which will stimulate the future, bring the external world in and help the business learn from this by experimenting. Good leadership looks to create an environment where only necessary work gets done. They manage meaning by the way they communicate and encourage people to tell the truth.

In some ways the hardest issue in Asia is to get people to speak the truth, in public, about how they feel. We have borrowed tools which have helped here like the "Great Debate" because this unleashes passion and this is when the truth gets spoken.

One other practice I heard of was done by one of our senior leaders. It was not in UFS but reflects the practice of bringing the outside world in. On arriving in a country where we had a strong market position, she wanted to energize the company to do better. She asked some large local investors (who normally do start-ups) to review the company plans and decide if they would invest in their company plan if they had one million dollars. After the review they said no and why. The plan was then revised until they would invest. It got better!

How Teams Work

Teams require a common direction and good interaction. They do not automatically work well and often it seems to be a collection of individuals. As one commentator described a great football team:

Great teams are far from cozy. I am sure many of you played in strong sporting teams; perhaps sat in changing rooms after losing. The weak team mopes, the strong team tears each other to pieces, analyzes all the mistakes, excuses nothing and resolves to put it right, trains with renewed vigor and . . . wins next week.

Often, leadership focuses on individuals. It is important because closeness to individuals is often hard in large, spread-out organizations but it is not sufficient to answer the question of "How good can we be?" Leadership needs to focus on key teams to make sure they expand their capabilities, increase their diversity, and pay particular attention to their dialogue. The quality of the dialogue, challenge and support is a good test of the health of the team.

What is clear is that if a country which has very good practices in one area and goes through the discipline of what it takes to achieve this and get growth, other countries will then adopt the same practices to help them achieve their own tough growth targets. But two aspects are key—tough growth targets and the way that the dialogue is held within the team.

But when people do good work they like to show it off. What matters even more than their bosses' approval is the approval and respect of their friends. As a final note, perhaps everybody likes to work for a fast-growing company, especially now in declining markets because **it is a public advertisement of how good we can be**.

Endnotes

1. This article represents the personal views of Fergus Balfour and does not represent those of Unilever.

CHAPTER 12

Leadership Challenges, Opportunities and Strategies for New Asia— The TCS Approach

Girija Pande

The business environment we face today is increasingly complex, dynamic and fraught with uncertainties. As an IT company headquartered in India and operating with a global workforce of over 143,000 consultants in 42 countries, Tata Consultancy Services (TCS) faces leadership and talent management challenges brought about by worldwide demographic trends, developments in the IT industry and the uniqueness of the Asian corporate and talent landscape. This paper shares how TCS seeks to overcome these challenges.

A Global Snapshot

With increased globalization in the twenty-first century, the ripple effects of macro-economic changes have had significant impact on international markets.

■ *211* ■

Take for instance the IT sector: our heavy reliance on the banking sector and dependence on the US market has certainly impacted us. However, despite the downturn, TCS grew 23 percent year on year, demonstrating agility and strong leadership. Technology and innovation continue to be the critical drivers for business. And from the turbulence will emerge new opportunities, which will recreate the future.

Faster Shift of Jobs from the West to the East

As multinationals and other business corporations face the brunt of shrinking income, they would actively seek to leverage the skilled labor markets of Asia. Higher quality, lower operating costs and the availability of an educated workforce will certainly fuel the increase in IT business opportunities and IT jobs.

Global IT Spending Will Hold Despite the Economic Slowdown

Despite forecasting a fall in global IT spending, the Economist Intelligence Unit (EIU) asserts that the purported drop will be below the general spending decline. The EIU's Report said the IT industry is diverse and robust enough worldwide to guarantee areas of growth.

At TCS, there are four important demographic trends which we think will shape our workforce of the twenty-first century.

1) Cultural Diversity

Increasing cultural diversity will be the characteristic of our global workforce. There are more than 10,000 professionals at TCS from 67 nationalities and it is not uncommon for workforce teams from diverse cultural backgrounds working in virtual teams across different continents.

2) Gender Balance

The steadily increasing participation of women in the workforce is certainly correcting the gender imbalance. Currently, 30 percent of TCS' over 143,000 employees worldwide are women. Women graduates are on the rise both in developing and developed countries. This requires adjustments in policies by organizations to accommodate the needs and expectations of the diverse workforce.

3) The Aging Population

The falling birth rates in developed countries, like Japan and Singapore, and other countries worldwide have two implications—the existing workforce needs to retire later and the existing gap needs to be filled, most probably by talent from other parts of the world. As a result of population aging and the increased participation of women, another dimension of change is that more workers have responsibilities outside of work. Employers need to play a significant role in showing empathy towards these aspects which will be a key to retention.

4) Engaging Multiple Generations: The Influx of Gen Y

Generation Y, also known as millennials, are the fastest-growing segment of the workforce. Over the next four years, close to 10 million more Gen Y people will enter the workforce. Ironically, although their numbers parallel their parents' generation (the Baby Boomers), the similarity ends here: in almost every other way, Gen Y is very different. They are the first in history to have lived their entire lives with information technology (IT).

The IT Industry

The IT services industry has grown to US$1 trillion, employing millions of professionals worldwide. The leadership challenges faced by IT organizations have these unique characteristics:

1) Knowledge-Based Industry

The IT industry is knowledge-based and its most important asset is its intellectual capital. Intellectual capital comprises human capital and intellectual assets—the latter being any reusable knowledge or expertise.

2) The IT industry is a service industry

Apart from the technical skills that the professionals have to offer, consulting skills such as client and people management skills are becoming increasingly important to partner with businesses at a strategic level. Innovation, sound business acumen and expertise in conceptualizing and delivering solutions are the key differentiators for TCS in a highly competitive environment.

3) Extremely fast paced

There is perhaps no other industry in the world that requires reskilling and growth in new competencies as in IT. The breathtaking pace at which the IT industry moves keeps employees and management alike under constant pressure to maintain leadership and offer the benefits of cutting-edge technology to its global customers.

In the context of this global and industry-specific environment that we operate in, TCS faces unique leadership challenges in Asia. The following deliberation outlines these challenges and TCS' response to it.

Challenges Faced in Asia

1) Management of Diversity

Diversity: Different cultures and nationalities

Effective employee communication and engagement are critical success factors as the workforce continues to expand globally and becomes multicultural. The organizational capability to nurture and maintain effective intercultural dialogue through active employee engagement programs is imperative. Statistically, over three quarters of international acquisitions and alliances fail due to cultural differences.

Diversity: Engaging the Baby Boomers, Gen X and Gen Y

Apart from the more apparent cultural and nationality differences that we need to overcome, the generational difference within the workforce further adds a layer of complexity to this challenge.

The average age of employees in most of the Asian IT companies is about 25 years. We are engaging with a very young and vibrant group of employees. They are typically in the operational roles, directly engaging with the clients and enabling them to reap benefits through IT-enabled processes and systems.

However, the tactical and strategic leadership layer generally consists of employees from Gen X and the Baby Boomer's era. Taking into consideration the margins of error for such stereotypical groupings, ample evidence has emerged to suggest that trends in mindsets, expectations, needs and approaches of each generation are quite different from the other.

To maximize employee productivity and satisfaction (of both customers and employees), it is of critical importance to nurture and engage this highly diverse team. If managed effectively from the leadership perspective, this will become a competitive advantage rather than a liability.

2) Learning to Work with Adversity: Paradigms of New Technologies, Skills Changes, While Leveraging on Opportunities

The IT industry is characterized by speed, competitiveness and breakthrough technologies. This challenge can be summed up as the inevitable need to be agile as a business organization. Organizations need to proactively embrace change while retaining core competencies and values.

Key to the success are in ensuring an organization's strategy, frameworks and that people are agile enough to recognize and respond to the changing business environ-ment with speed. This is of essence to the customers that we support.

3) Leadership

In our business, intellectual capital is our most important asset and human resources the single most important competitive differentiator. Given the scale, rate of our growth and expansion, developing leaders for the future is not an option but is necessary for the success of the business.

A leader is characterized by his or her ability to spot potential new ideas that will create new growth levers for the organization. With increasing commoditization of IT services, customers need to perceive added value to engage with an organization. The leader's role is to clearly define this value proposition and consistently communicate it to all key stakeholders in the business.

4) *Attracting and Retaining Talent*

Attracting and retaining talent continues to be a major challenge. Gartner[1] has reported that the average tenure for an IT professional in an organization is less than three years. Rather than a heftier paycheck, opportunities to work in new technologies, scope for professional learning, career development and a challenging environment rank higher in priorities.

TCS Strategic Responses

TCS is addressing these challenges through multiple strategies. These strategies are formulated and implemented with TCS core values and best practices at its foundation.

Agile Business Model

Agility is about high-performing organizations. Every agile organization raises its performance bar to help its customers improve their efficiencies and come out of this meltdown stronger.

To attain higher agility and identify the levers that will make its customers stronger, TCS adopted the Tata Business

Excellence Model (TBEM) (see Figure 12.1). TBEM incorporates the aspects of Corporate Governance as provided in the Malcolm Baldrige criteria 2007.

This model helps in providing a timely, structured and focused feedback through objective assessments and criteria to the leadership team. TBEM criteria help TCS to use an integrated approach to organizational performance management that results in:

- Delivery of ever improving value to TCS customers and stakeholders, contributing to organizational sustainability
- Improvement of overall organizational effectiveness and capabilities
- Organization and personal learning

The core values and concepts embodied in the criteria are as follows:

- Leadership
- Strategic Planning
- Customer and Market Focus
- Measurement, Analysis and Knowledge Management
- Workforce Focus
- Process Management
- Business Results

Leadership, Strategic Planning, and Customer and Market Focus represent the leadership triad. The senior leaders set organizational direction and seek future opportunities for the organization.

Workforce Focus, Process Management and Business Results represent the results triad. The organization's workforce and key processes accomplish the work of the organization that yields overall performance results.

FIGURE 12-1. TATA BUSINESS EXCELLENCE MODEL (TBEM)

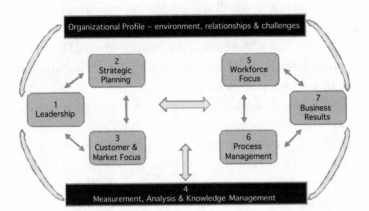

All actions point towards results—a composite of product and service, customer and market, financial and internal operational performance results, including workforce, leadership, governance and social responsi-bility results.

Measurement, Analysis and Knowledge Management are critical to the effective management of organization and to a fact-based, knowledge-driven system for improving performance and competitiveness. They serve as the foundation for the ongoing organizational performance management.

TCS became the world's first organization to achieve an Integrated Enterprise-wide Maturity Level 5 on both Capability Maturity Model and People Capability Maturity Model.

Think Long Term, No Short Cuts

TCS continues to invest in future trends. Sustainability, Green IT and Cloud Computing are areas of opportunity which TCS will leverage. The Cloud Computing–based IT services model for small and medium enterprises, currently being piloted in India, is an example of a business model innovation that will set a new precedence in the IT industry. Such initiatives can be replicated, once they are mature, into multiple global markets.

TCS has always adapted quickly to changing circumstances by its responsive and creative thinking. For customers, it presents an enviable value proposition enabled by four decades of experience, domain knowledge, technology excellence and offerings of full services play. It has focused on moving up the value chain from IT Outsourcing → Full Services → Business Services.

In the Asia-Pacific region, TCS is well poised to gain advantage from newer areas such as Healthcare, Energy, Utilities and Telecommunications including the impact of new technologies such as broadband, 3G, WiMAX, LTE and others. It continues to be an engine of growth because of its proven ability to reinvent the organization and the business.

Talent and Leadership Grooming

The company's greatest asset is its young workforce whose energy and vitality permeates beyond TCS into the community, through employee engagement channels like Maitree, which offers youngsters the opportunity to contribute in different areas of community well-being, such as education, healthcare and conservation.

TCS worldwide, over 1.6 million learning days have been invested in developing additional competencies in 2008–09, around 23,000 TCSers gained additional technology certifications. We believe that creating talent readiness will drive agility in learning and development.

TCS continues to expand its Web-based learning program to benefit its diverse workforce. New e-learning modules have been launched in Portuguese, Mandarin and Spanish to help employees in Latin America and China develop their competencies. New initiatives are in the pipeline that will speed up these efforts. A new integration portal has been launched. This is designed to familiarize and educate people on the values, ethos and culture of the organization, especially for those who have newly joined the company. Additionally, there is enhanced focus on cross training for experienced professionals in the organization to ensure continuous improvement in utilization.

The attrition rate of 11.4 percent (previous year 12.6 percent) in fiscal 2009 is the lowest in the industry. This lowest attrition rate has been achieved by continuously investing in learning and development programs for employees, competitive compensation, creating a compelling work environment, empowering employees at all levels as well as a well-structured reward and recognition mechanism.

In the Asian market, we have alliances with leading universities in Australia to attract and recruit talented Information and Communication Technologies (ICT) graduates. Concurrently, a strong talent localization initiative led to the rapid increase of our local headcount, including the 1,200 employees currently in China, creating a multi-lingual, multicultural global organization.

Leadership Development

At the organization-wide level there are focused and sustained initiatives to develop future leaders. These programs are designed to identify, nurture and develop leadership through:

(i) Intensive classroom-based experiential learning which is achieved through experience sharing of current senior leaders in the organization.

(ii) Focused behavioral/functional training depending on their expected roles.

(iii) Specific on-the-job training by assigning them to special assignments to develop their competencies in new areas identified based on their competency assessment and learning gaps.

(iv) An institutionalized mentoring program called PEEP (Proactive Employee Engagement Program) where the mentee is mentored by senior leaders through a structured mentoring program facilitated by HR.

The Hi-Po Initiative (High Potential Initiative) is one such initiative where promising talent and potential leaders are first identified in accordance with well-defined TCS' leadership criteria. At present, about 30 percent of TCS associates are covered.

What Does This Achieve?

1) Establishment of Rapport = Increased Job Satisfaction

The proactive interaction between the senior management and employees help establish rapport and open up channels for communication. This results in increased job satisfaction and overall well-being of the potential leader.

2) Two-Way Knowledge Transfer

The knowledge transfer between the mentors and mentee is also beneficial to both parties; on the one hand, the mentee gains experience, guidance and increased exposure while borrowing a bird's eye perspective of the mentor. The mentor, on the other hand, gleans on-the-ground, real-time information pertaining to trends and workings from the perspective of the mentee.

Leveraging Limitations

We are going through a very difficult phase. The crisis in the financial sector led to a lower confidence in financial markets leading to a global credit crunch. The past year has witnessed some of the sharpest falls in both financial marketplace and the industrial economy. According to the International Monetary Fund (IMF) World Economic Outlook 2009, the advanced economies declined by 7.5 percent in real GDP during the third quarter of the last fiscal year. Although the US economy was among the hardest hit, this also had its cascading effect on economies in both Western Europe and Asia.

The cascading effect on the emerging economies was partially driven by lower confidence on these economies, resulting in capital flight from these economies to developed economies and contraction of global trade. The uncertainties in the markets led to significant volatility in exchange rates as well as commodity prices.

These events led to a set of rapid fiscal and monetary policy responses from governments across the globe. Responses included fiscal stimulus packages across various economies, coordinated efforts by central banks worldwide to lower interest rates, injections of liquidity into financial markets including quantitative easing.

IMF indicates that overall world economic growth is likely to decline by 1.3 percent in 2009 and would recover in 2010. However, the growth and revival process is expected to be slow. The Indian and Chinese economies, nevertheless, are expected to grow at 5 and 7 percent respectively during 2009.

To address these challenges, TCS, which already has a wide presence both in developed and in emerging markets, has taken the following steps:

- Increasing the breadth and depth of service offerings and penetration of new customer accounts and markets to combat slowdown in some customer segments.
- To lower the operating costs of its global clientele, TCS is increasing the leverage of low-cost locations in Asia.
- Increasing the localization of its workforce.
- Encouraging innovation through various forums and increasing the employee engagement at all levels.

Despite its size, TCS has stayed true to its roots of building collaborative models of development, reaching out and expanding its ecosystem to work together with partners, venture capitalists, academia and the Government in order to innovate for its stakeholders. These reflect the new models of innovation where global teams work virtually to create and build new solutions and ideas. Being at the hub of this ecosystem, TCS has been able to leverage these relationships to build a network of Innovation Labs and create new solutions to address customer pain points.

The TCS Brand

"Experience Certainty": Over the years, the TCS brand has become synonymous with "Experience Certainty" and this is fully endorsed by customers. Customers value the assurance of getting their unique requirements met on time, within budget and with high quality. This makes them more responsive to the business with better efficiency and enables them to shift investment to strategic initiatives rather than tactical functions.

The solid reputation TCS has built over the years will serve the company well as customers would be more willing to derive contracts, even in emerging areas of new technologies, with a recognized and trusted name. This is one of TCS' greatest strengths, which, alongside its other technical capabilities and abilities (with regard to technicalities), will allow TCS to leverage fully on the opportunities available.

TCS Financial Strength

Acquisition Power: Financial strength, coupled with the additional financial capability derived from a large market capitalization, gives TCS an enviable acquisition capability. TCS' financial might, especially in the context of these troubled financial times, allows TCS the buffer and flexibility to fully utilize this resource to enable even more sustainable growth for the organization.

TCS Unique Products and Services

Integrated Full Services Capabilities: Our ability to provide integrated services continues to present an exciting value proposition to global customers. This offering encompasses the entire value chain of IT, from consulting, developing solutions and products, to implementation and support.

Operating Model for Driving Future Growth: The operating model adopted by TCS is the driver for future growth and will help move TCS to the next level of performance.

TCS Strategic Competency Management

TCS emphasizes much on competency building and managing initiatives to nurture our human capital with an enterprise vision and strategy to address the growing scale and complexity of our global operations and customer expectations. This allows us to keep in line with fast-changing, on-the-ground trends, and make adjustments swiftly and appropriately to keep in time with the world's pendulum.

Looking towards the future, the philosophies of leadership, delivery excellence and the promise of "Experience certainty" are pillars on which the success of TCS is cemented. This is perhaps best reflected in the fact that, as a US$6 billion company, TCS has achieved its vision of being counted among the top ten IT services companies in the world today.

As organizations continue to operate and compete in a dynamic global scenario where unpredictability is the norm, winning organizations need to convert today's challenges into tomorrow's opportunities. It is this belief that fuels TCS' commitment to invest in building people competencies and ensure human capital development on an unparalleled scale.

TCS has grown globally across mature markets (NA, EU) as well as in new growth markets (Asia Pacific, Middle East, Latin America and India). TCS' full services capabilities (IT Services, Infrastructure, BPO, Assurance and Consulting) have expanded and fueled growth. All key verticals including BFSI, manufacturing and retail, posted double-digit growth, and TCS continues to grow its industry capabilities and expertise to ensure both technology and industry prowess.

TCS continues to be an engine of growth because of its proven ability to reinvent the organization and the business, its ability to work in a collaborative mode, to learn constantly, to critically evaluate all that it does and demonstrate the leadership it is known for.

Endnote

1. Gartner Inc., "New Compensation Study Reveals That More Than Half of IT Professionals Leave Their Employers Within Three Years." July 31, 2001.

CHAPTER 13

Sustainable Talent Development at Microsoft

Jessica Tan Soon Neo

The Past 30 Years

As a software company, Microsoft's core assets are centered on our people. Intellectual Property (IP) is our business. IP can be driven only by one thing, brain power and the ability to get software into the hands of people and businesses that can benefit from it on a global scale. It sounds simple, but it clearly is not if you think about the diverse number of customer business problems we are trying to solve, economic background and maturity to deal with, geographic reach and the increased complexity of scaling the effort through third parties like our partner ecosystem.

As a company, we believe strongly in the magic of our software. Not just from an innovation standpoint, but also in how we go to market, how we make technology affordable for the masses so we can help realize potential in all four corners of the world, regardless of economic standing or business. It has taken us 30 years to put technology into the hands of more than one billion people.

The next challenge is to do this for the next five billion people. To answer this challenge, the question we constantly ask ourselves is, "What are the skills of the leaders and the people that we need to get us there?" Clearly, this calls for a sustainable approach to managing our business and our people, even in a small country like Singapore.

The Need for a Sustainable Approach

Microsoft's 30-year history has seen tremendous growth and change, from a fledgling start-up company, to one with multiple businesses and, as a result, an ever-growing competitive landscape. Through acquisitions, organic growth and product extensions, the company is, today, a highly complex one. The industry and Microsoft's business in Asia Pacific is also going through significant change as we speak—from the myriad software we bring to market, the way services are delivered, our partner ecosystem and the customer segments which we serve. How do we ensure we are moving in the same direction, led by the same values, and remaining true to the intent of enabling individuals, communities and businesses through technology?

As a company, we are constantly faced with the challenge of being a culture in transition. Because of the nature of innovation in technology, we will always have pockets of people who think they are in a start-up. Then you have a group of people who have seen the company through thick and thin. Over the years, Microsoft has also hired people who have worked with established businesses. All these have resulted in us having to constantly manage our changing value propositions, even to our employees.

The current economic environment has also accelerated some of these changes and, to some extent, has led to Microsoft making its very first decision to reduce global headcount by 5,000 over 18 months in February 2009. This is unprecedented in Microsoft's history—we did not see this level of impact during the dot-com bust. However, this has more to do with how we want to evolve as a company with new leadership, new technologies and new ways of serving our customers.

All these mean that it is all the more important for us to focus on ensuring that our employees are engaged, are aware of the context for change and are equipped with the necessary development to take on new challenges. Despite the economic downturn, we continue to invest in developing our best people and equipping them with the best technologies to enable them to do their best work. Tough times require a more productive and smarter workforce. Training and career development con-tinue to be critical areas to ensure the future success of our company.

Hence the need for a sustainable and consistent approach to talent acquisition, development, retention and ensuring we have a healthy pipeline of leaders.

Five-Pillar People Strategy

Over the last five years, Microsoft's leadership and human resources have led the development of an integrated approach to talent management. These include having a consistent framework throughout the globe which we call myMicrosoft (see Figure 13.1). This is a critical part of our People Management Rhythm in Microsoft.

FIGURE 13-1. THE FIVE SUPPORTING PILLARS OF MYMICROSOFT

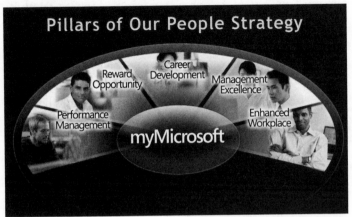

myMicrosoft is a broad set of investments designed for performance management, reward, recognition, career development opportunities, equipping managers with leadership skills and ensuring we have a conducive environment for people to do their best work. It is our ultimate goal to ensure that Microsoft continues to be one of the world's best places to work in the countries which we operate.

myMicrosoft has five supporting pillars which constitute the focus areas critical to employees and the success of our business:

1. Performance Management

One of our core beliefs at Microsoft is that our future success depends on all of us making others great. Performance management at Microsoft is an integral part of our overall talent management cycle which comprises two key events—Annual Performance Review and Mid-year Career Discussion (see Figure 13.2).

It is an ongoing process by which we manage and develop our most important resource: our people. Setting commitments, giving feedback, coaching, developing and rewarding employees for their performance not only form the basis of our performance management process but these also help our employees do their best work. Throughout the year, this process is supported by regular one-on-one meetings between managers and employees to ensure ongoing dialogue about the employees' progress on their commitments and business priorities. Our systems and tools are also in place to support these and assist both manager and employee to track progress and impact.

FIGURE 13-2. MICROSOFT'S OVERALL TALENT MANAGEMENT CYCLE

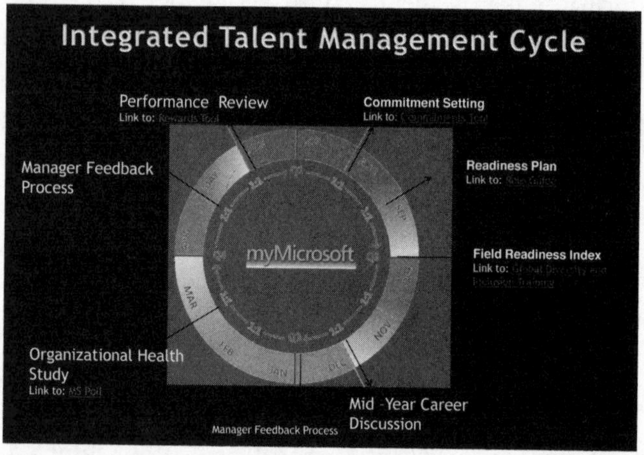

2. Reward Portfolio

We have a long-standing philosophy of pay for performance. We believe in fostering an environment that rewards

our employees for doing their best work to drive business results. Our objective is to attract, develop and retain key talent by delivering the highest compensation to the highest performing employees over the course of their career.

Our compensation programs are built on four key principles, as Table 13.1 shows.

TABLE 13-1. THE FOUR KEY PRINCIPLES OF MICROSOFT'S COMPENSATION PROGRAMS

Distinctiveness	Differentiation	Accountability	Market Competitiveness
•Microsoft strives to be a leader in offering a total reward package that is distinctive in a competitive environment	•The Microsoft reward programs enable meaningful reward differentiation based on performance and anticipated future contributions	•Microsoft holds managers accountable for assessing employee performance and recommending fiscally sound, differentiated cash and stock rewards	•Microsoft has employees in over 100 countries throughout the world and offers competitive cash and stock compensation relative to those markets

3. Management Excellence

The overall success of Microsoft is directly tied to the critical role that our managers play. Managers shape the success of our teams by driving business results and helping employees realize their full potential. Management Excellence (ME) is one of the five myMicrosoft pillars. The ME vision is to be a magnet for managers who want to develop themselves to attract, develop and retain top global talent.

By creating a climate where people can succeed and thrive, managers help ensure that Microsoft continues to be one of the world's best places to work. This is especially important as we move to an increasingly distributed and globally dispersed workforce and as Microsoft continues to expand in key regions.

So, how do we help our leaders and managers develop exceptional people and build sustainable businesses? At Microsoft, our managers ride through our Management Excellence (ME) roadmap which covers Continuous Learning (e.g., management skills training, focus on manager competencies, mentoring, best practices sharing) and Community Connections (ME Community). The community connection is key to developing our managers through leveraging different experiences and bringing learning to life on the job.

Learning Circles (LE) is one way in which Microsoft instills a culture of learning from one another through network and connection.

The concept of Learning Circles is fairly straightforward to understand. It is in close conformance with state-of-the-art principles of adult learning. Its power is in its simplicity.

- A typical feature of a Learning Circle will consist of a small, close network of five to eight members (of similar work role and business priorities) who come together to share and learn together through both regular meetings and interactions.
  - For example, I belong to the Country Managers' Learning Circle with members of my Learning Circle being Country Managers like myself who have a similar market size and economic development.

- At the meetings, members get time in the Circle meeting to obtain help from other members to address his or her priorities and to identify relevant and realistic actions to take between meetings to address his or her priority.

The concept of Learning Circles has helped Microsoft mirror how today's leaders work and learn.

Today's business leaders face complex challenges. Day-to-day leadership challenges are seldom addressed by carefully chosen, well-structured and highly rational approaches to problem solving. Leaders do not always have the time to plan for each challenge. Instead, leaders often resort to highly intuitive, real-time approaches that are based on learning from their past experiences and help from others in the organization.

Effective leaders have "learned how to learn." This means they have developed the ability to closely examine their own perceptions, conclusions and actions. They have used that insight to more fully understand their day-to-day challenges, including what works and what does not work to address those challenges. Learning Circles are based on an adult learning and problem-solving process called Action Learning, which very closely matches the real world of today's leaders. As a result, the Learning Circles process helps members develop and practice leadership and problem-solving skills that can very quickly be applied in the workplace.

From a different angle, our ME approach does not just focus on the development of our managers. It also provides a holistic view on all the elements that drive and impact our managers. Table 13.2 shows the six distinct elements of the ME framework.

TABLE 13-2. MICROSOFT MANAGEMENT EXCELLENCE FRAMEWORK

Management Excellence Framework	
Clarify	A manager's clarity and conviction of their role and responsibility in ME. The Career Model and Performance Management teams are key partners in this element. *Examples: The Career Model and commitment setting*
Select	Tools to inform and assist in the selection of managers based on manager competencies. The staffing organization plays an integral role in the selection of our people managers. *Example: Exploring Management curriculum*
Assess	Assessment tools used to determine manager proficiency levels of manager competencies (based on feedback from others). The MS Poll, Performance Management and Career Model teams are partners in this element. *Examples: MS Poll, Career Compass and Microsoft 360*
Develop	The Core Offerings, Connections and Continuous Learning opportunities that help managers develop themselves to attract, develop and retain top global talent. The ME Team partners heavily with the Diversity and Inclusion organization for rich development opportunities and the HR line for needs assessment and feedback. *Examples: Foundation Event, Community and Electives*
Measure	Standards to evaluate a manager's effectiveness in ME. HR Business Partners and the Compensation and Benefits team are critical to this element. *Examples: Manager commitment and manager feedback*
Recognition	Recognition for managers who demonstrate the behaviors that result in ME. HR Business Partners and Compensation and Benefits are key to this element. *Example: Division-specific Management Excellence recognition*

4. Career Development

At Microsoft, we encourage our employees to develop to their full potential when it comes to career development. We believe the success of our career depends largely on ourselves—the time and energy we put on career and professional development. Microsoft's role in this aspect is to provide the environment and infrastructure for our people to pursue their career passions.

We have an integrated tool called Career Compass, a self-service Web-based tool that allows an employee to track and chart his or her career aspirations and development plans all in one place and at his or her own pace. See Figure 13.3.

FIGURE 13-3. MICROSOFT'S CAREER DEVELOPMENT MODELS AND TOOLS

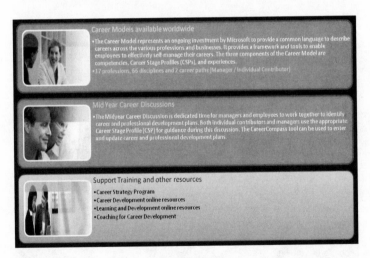

We also have our unique career language (note: not programming language) that we use globally to describe our career stages. This allows us to have a consistent framework

that assists in moving our talents around the world through job opportunities. This is essential in highly competitive and diverse markets that we operate in. It also provides our employees the exposure they desire to build their careers.

There are two career paths available at Microsoft: the individual contributor path and the manager path, and there are defined career stages on each path. Microsoft draws our leaders from both paths. Our employees decide on their own career options to excel as individual contributors or as managers. Their career aspirations are then built on whether they want to go deep or broad in the career option they have chosen. Microsoft has opportuni-ties across business units and functions to fulfill multiple paths. See Figure 13.4.

FIGURE 13-4. MICROSOFT CAREER PATHS

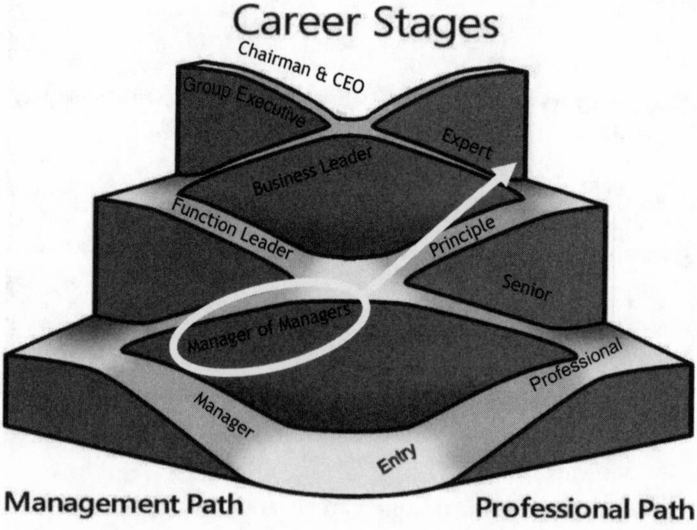

Career Stages

Chairman & CEO
Group Executive
Business Leader
Function Leader
Manager of Managers
Manager

Expert
Principle
Senior
Professional
Entry

Management Path   **Professional Path**

5. *Enhanced Workplace*

Our goal is to offer a world-class work environment that promotes innovation, productivity and greater work-life balance. Broadly, we categorize our initiatives into the following:

Sustainability Services: Microsoft continues our environmental efforts by introducing more initiatives that are focused on solving environmental challenges, reducing the company's carbon footprint, and altering what is being put into the waste stream, e.g., Earth Day.

Workplace Global Fund: This fund provides global Microsoft offices access to a fixed corporate budget that allows global Microsoft offices (e.g., better meeting room and conferencing facilities) and sites access to subsidies for enhanced commute, beverage and food programs. In Singapore, we provide daily fruits, healthy fruit juices and biscuits as part of the initiative to promote healthy eating. For those who crave for a crunch, there is fresh fruit every day and a wide variety range of healthy nuts to look forward to every Friday.

Employee Volunteer Program: To support and encourage our employees' dedication, passion and creativity in the community, Microsoft offers volunteering benefits and tools designed to help the communities they support through our citizenship efforts, e.g., paid volunteer days that enable employees to offer their services to worthy charitable causes and help people in need. Throughout the year, our employees in Singapore participate in various volunteer initiatives to help those in need.

I believe the journey through these five pillars has allowed you to appreciate how Microsoft invests in these areas to attract and retain the best talent in the market. For the individuals, all these pillars come together into creating one's experience of working in Microsoft, which we believe in turn creates the employee engagement to drive business results.

Grooming the Next Generation of Asian Leaders at Microsoft

Potential leaders are identified very early on in our people review process. Regardless of whether they take the professional or a management path, like me, leaders are assessed on four key areas: People Leadership, Organization Leadership, Business Leadership and Thought Leadership (see Figure 13.5).

FIGURE 13-5. MICROSOFT LEADERSHIP FRAMEWORK

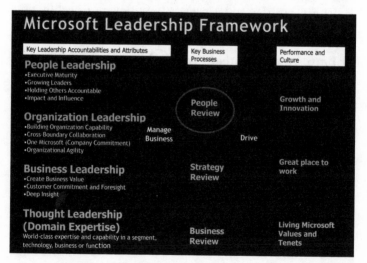

The framework is comprehensive and provides clear definitions around leadership competencies based on whether they are developing, fully developed or exceptional in each area of development. This process minimizes subjectivity through clear definitions. This also enables consistency in grooming leadership qualities and DNA that matter to us as a company for our sustained survival.

The Country Managers' Role and Succession Planning

To enable our people to be ready for career opportunities and available for career moves while ensuring business continuity, Succession Planning is an important focus for our business.

A Succession Plan is reviewed as a key part of our Annual Business Review Rhythm by Country, Area and Corporate Leadership to ensure currency and viability of the Plans. The Succession Plans cover all key leadership positions and the slate for talent that is "ready now" as well as "one to three moves away."

Future Direction and Concerns

From this discussion, I hope that I have been able to give a perspective of our mission. We may well take more than 30 years to reach the next five billion people. Ours is a knowledge-based industry that will scale only by touching people's lives directly. We do this through our employees, our business partners, the developer community, our partners in social responsibility and, more recently, through social networking. Hence, capacity building will always be a key priority for us.

Our diverse business challenges need to be mirrored by the diversity of people we employ and work with both within our organization and through the ecosystem.

We believe we have an evolved and mature framework which will equip us with the necessary guidance to address talent retention. But the usual challenges of hiring the right people, a strong leadership pipeline and diversity will continue to challenge us in every market in which we operate in Asia.

When I took on the role of Managing Director for Microsoft Singapore almost 12 months ago, I set the vision of making Microsoft Singapore a breeding ground for talent and a net exporter of talent. It is only when we are able to bring the best talents to work at Microsoft and allow them to do their best work that we will be able to deliver the value and impact of our technology and innovation to our customers and partners.

Having a vibrant IT talent base and ecosystem is vital to the success of the industry in any economy and hence the need to build capacity. As a company that operates a business that touches the lives of people and businesses from all walks of life, we must rely heavily on our partner ecosystem. Today, we already invest in a continuum of programs, from primary schools to start-ups and software developers. We believe that this will nurture talent for the local software economy. It is from this vast pool of talent that we hope will form the talent base to help build and contribute to Singapore's mission to be a hub for the InfoComm industry. It will also provide a healthy source of talent for Microsoft and our partners.

If I may do a little star gazing on this: I believe that there is huge potential for us to groom the next generation of InfoComm leaders, not just for Singapore, but also as future global InfoComm leaders. Here is where I, as the country leader for the company, must dare to think big and ask the questions about the role that Singapore can play and help build the ecosystem to support this dream:

1. Is Singapore a good place to attract, retain and develop the best talent for Microsoft and our partners?
2. How can we in Singapore be a global leader within the Microsoft community, to champion the causes that we work hard to achieve?
3. The diversity at Microsoft has already seen strong talent from China, India, France, UK, Germany, Australia and even a small country like Belgium make the senior management rungs at the Microsoft Corporation. How can the next Ray Ozzie (Chief Software Architect from Microsoft, who has just replaced Bill Gates) come from Singapore?

This is a journey and we may take some time to achieve our goal. But I believe that we must start and continue to invest and build our talent base. It is not about getting it right from the word go. It is about taking a longer-term view, having big bets, investing, innovating, and improving processes and ideas as we go along in order to realize the impact of our focus on people.

CHAPTER 14

Positive Leadership

Gerald Chan

Given the challenges of today's business environment and the outlook of the markets, there are two key aspects of leadership that I believe will be the deciding factors to help Asian firms ride out this recession. The first is "positive leadership" or the ability to lead oneself during times of crisis. The second is "talent engagement"—the ability to keep one's talents engaged, committed and resilient during difficult times.

Who We Are

Headquartered in Zurich and Basel, Switzerland, UBS is one of the world's leading financial firms. It serves a discerning, international client base with its wealth management, investment banking and asset management businesses. In Switzerland, UBS is the market leader in retail and commercial banking.

■ *244* ■

UBS is present in all major financial centers worldwide. It has offices in over 50 countries, with about 38 percent of its employees working in the Americas, 34 percent in Switzerland, 15 percent in the rest of Europe and 13 percent in Asia Pacific. UBS employs more than 75,000 people around the world. Its shares are listed on the SIX Swiss Exchange, the New York Stock Exchange (NYSE) and the Tokyo Stock Exchange (TSE).

UBS has had a presence in Singapore since the 1970s through the Union Bank of Switzerland and Swiss Bank Corporation. Following the global merger between the two banks in June 1998, UBS is now a leading foreign financial institution in Singapore, with over 2,200 employees covering the Wealth Management, Investment Bank and Global Asset Management businesses. Singapore is a wealth management hub for UBS and the South Asian headquarters for investment banking. Singapore, together with Hong Kong, is also one of the two primary wealth management booking centers in Asia Pacific.

Singapore is also where we house our UBS Wealth Management Campus for Asia Pacific, which was opened in April 2007. The Campus provides training for employees new to the wealth management industry and ongoing training and professional development for existing UBS employees. The Campus underpins UBS's commitment to nurture and groom the best talent in Asia.

Positive Leadership

Let me now share my views on the two aspects of leadership, "positive leadership" and "talent engagement," which I mentioned in the opening paragaph of this article. As we chart our course by adapting to the ever-changing financial landscape, it is important to take destiny in our own hands and have the resilience to carry on and persevere towards a common goal of building a stronger firm.

One of the key UBS values is the ability to lead oneself and maintain positive leadership. This is not easy, especially in the past 18 months, with markets remaining depressed and as the world continues to head towards one of the worst recessions of our times.

We recognize that when times are difficult, emotional and mental stress levels increase. At UBS Singapore, we provide our employees with support initiatives such as Work-Life Coaching where employees have access to counselors to help them through challenges, whether personal or work related. The access to counselors also extends to their immediate family members. as we believe in the importance of the family unit in relation to our employees' performance at work.

In addition, we regularly provide our employees with talks and events that focus on coping with stress, dealing with changes and their general well-being, including physical, mental and financial health. These events and talks are also open to the family members of our employees.

One recent initiative was a half-day workshop titled "The Science of Positive Leadership in Challenging Times." This workshop specifically dealt with the issue of positive leadership and provided the audience with the tools in changing our mindsets to becoming more positive. Shawn Achor graduated from the Harvard University and served as Head of Teaching Fellow for Dr. Tal Ben-Shahar's "Positive Psychology" class. Professor Achor utilizes his breakthrough research to enhance individual engagement and cultivate a more productive workplace. At the core of his work is the recent revolutionary finding that individual happiness and organizational success are inextricably linked. He reminded us that it is about training the mind to look at the positive and not at the negative, to choose to be happy. One of the tools he encouraged us to use is to maintain a daily journal of "gratitude." By focusing our minds on positive things that happened to us for us to feel gratitude, we condition our minds to immediately look out for a positive aspect of a situation that is confronting us. This habit will have a knock-on effect on each of us, both personally and professionally.

Positive Leadership, however, is not about being unrealistically optimistic. Jim Collins, in his book *Good to Great*, relates the story of Admiral James Stockdale who was shot down in Vietnam and was the highest ranking officer who was a prisoner of war for almost eight years. His strategy for coping during his imprisonment as a prisoner of war was that "You must never confuse faith that you will prevail in the end—which you can never afford to lose—with the discipline to confront the most brutal facts of your current reality, whatever they might be." In the current challenging times and recession we face, as a firm and as a member of the global economy, it is important that we do not doubt that we will ride this wave and survive it and that this experience will be our defining event. Our strong value of integrity and our culture of transparency lead us to continue making realistic assessments and focus our energies and strategies to better face each challenge as it comes so as to position ourselves with a stronger chance to prevail.

Anticipating and adapting to changes are part of the UBS's corporate culture as we strive to constantly improve on the quality and efficiency of existing processes to deliver the best service to our clients. The most recent annual employee survey showed that approximately 80 percent of our employee population reported that they are highly and personally motivated to contribute beyond what is expected of them. This result shows the continued dedication of our employees despite the challenges being faced to lead themselves and it certainly depicts the culture that we have built in the firm.

Talent Development and Engagement

UBS has a tradition and culture of talent development hotwired into our firm's DNA. We recognize the importance of our talent as the cornerstone of our firm's successful growth strategy. We ensure that all our employees are able to reach their full potential through a comprehensive talent development menu of programs.

In April 2007, we opened our UBS Wealth Management Campus for Asia Pacific here in Singapore. Our UBS Wealth Management Campus is a symbolic icon that reflects our continued emphasis on our employees' talent development. The Campus provides training for employees who are new to the wealth management industry as well as ongoing training and professional development for existing UBS employees. The Campus underpins UBS's commitment to nurture and groom the best talent in Asia. Through the Campus, our employees gain access to a comprehensive educational program delivered locally.

The UBS Wealth Management Campus dovetails with Singapore's efforts to develop a premier wealth management hub. It has benefited from Singapore's large pool of highly educated talent, a robust financial services sector, an open regulatory environment and the support of the Monetary Authority of Singapore (MAS) for such vocational education initiatives.

To adapt to the very challenging market and economic conditions over the past two years, it has been even more important to ensure that regular employee engagement efforts continue.

UBS Singapore has consistently been engaging employees on all levels over the years. Senior leaders of the firm welcome feedback and dialogue with employees and are accessible to employees of all levels for them to voice their ideas and concerns. Formal regular communication and updates are provided to employees, involving regional management, local management as well as senior leaders of the firm. I engage with middle management regularly in coffee sessions to share specifics of business strategy and announcements or results so that they in turn can share with their team members. This allows for a level of assurance among the talent population and provides them with a better sense of understanding of the firm's strategies and position. It, in turn, allows employees to feel more engaged.

We continue to provide programs that also focus on the "softer" side of the business, particularly in the personal development of our employees as individuals. We strive to provide them with the tools to do their job better and more effectively, to build their confidence and certainly to stretch their capacity so as to empower them in their career development and path.

Creating "Stickiness"

While UBS may have the infrastructure and all these programs in place, I have personally found that the winning formula of increasing employee engagement, of creating "stickiness" among our employees, and also their family members, is through programs that touch the heart. Our diversity and community affairs programs and initiatives have proven to be the heartbeat of UBS Singapore; as a firm, they are also two of our ethical beliefs by which we function as a business.

At UBS Singapore, we have actively engaged our employees from the onset that, as our human capital, they are one of our key assets. We strongly believe that one of the best ways to engage our employees is to embrace their diversity of skills, perspectives, thoughts and backgrounds.

Through our diversity programs, we are able to foster an inclusive corporate culture which is open-minded and based on meritocracy. This culture allows us to nurture the leadership potential among all our employees.

The business case behind diversity in the workforce is that it allows us to reach out to our increasingly sophisticated clients around the world. With a diversity of backgrounds and experiences from our diverse workforce in Singapore, we are better equipped and able to understand our clients and their needs and anticipate and create unique solutions for them.

The key in the embracing of diversity is in the building of a culture of working with respect. It is vital that all employees are comfortable with their backgrounds, perspectives, thoughts and skills and that they accept that these may be different from the person sitting in the next cubicle. We believe that the four cornerstones of embracing diversity are open-mindedness, teamwork, honesty and respect. At UBS, we let our differences make the difference.

It is especially heartening to see that our UBS Singapore colleagues have taken the initiative to give back to the community through a variety of creative community outreach efforts over the years.

UBS strongly believes in investing in the communities that we operate in. This stems from our sense of corporate responsibility as well as our holistic investment in not just our employees via all our various programs, but also in the communities that they belong to.

UBS Singapore's community affairs program has been in place for the past five or six years and during this time, we have endeavored to make a difference in the lives of the beneficiaries of the charity partners we have partnered. This program has served to not just impact the beneficiaries, but also forge strong bonds among our employees as they participate in the various initiatives to give back to the local community.

Volunteering is, of course, key in our efforts of giving back and it is firmly hotwired into the DNA of our culture, our business and our development programs. Our management leads by example in volunteering and as a management committee, members of that committee kick-start the year's program of volunteering. Our volunteering calendar includes projects that run regularly including daily, weekly and monthly activities, during business hours, ad-hoc weekend activities and projects that help build capacity in the charity sector. Employees of all levels are engaged, and frequently, family members of employees as well as business partners and vendors of UBS are also invited to participate alongside us.

Community investment does not end with volunteerism. Employees also rally together to raise funds for charity partners through a variety of ways. UBS Singapore Day is a day that we set aside to acknowledge the talents of our employees that are not work-related via a Talent Quest as well as recognize members of the staff who, as nominated by their colleagues for a UBS Singapore CEO Award, have either made an impact as an external ambassador of UBS to the community or an internal one within the firm. Audience members of the Talent Quest vote for their favorite performance by making donations, and all monies collected are donated to charity. In addition to the UBS Singapore Talent Quest, a separate talent contest invites "auction bids" for certain senior members of the staff to perform and all bids are donated to charity. These efforts exemplify our employees' commitment to our community affairs philosophy. The beneficiaries of our charity partners are also frequently invited to participate in staff events—for our employees and their family members, these activities further cement our philosophy and respect.

UBS also encourages personal philanthropy among employees by matching the personal donations they have made to charities of their choice, within certain set parameters. This ability of choice empowers our employees to make a difference in a charitable cause that they feel for and it is just another way that UBS demonstrates our commitment to our employees.

Conclusion

Our continued commitment to our employees through the years, in so many different ways, has built a strong foundation of engagement. It has, in turn, built a culture of camaraderie that speaks for itself, and despite all the challenges UBS and our employees are facing, and the current economic crisis, it is inspiring that our employees are dedicated in doing their best at this time, in the strong belief that it will put them, and the firm, in the best place for the upturn.

We believe that consant engagement with our employees and positive leadership are key as we continue to chart our destiny with resilience and perseverance, and continue building a stronger firm. In the words of Henry Ford: "Coming together is a beginning, keeping together is progress and working together is success."

CHAPTER **15**

Leadership Challenges in Asia
Integration and Next Steps

Dave Ulrich

This outstanding volume of essays offers a rich glimpse at current and future leadership challenges in the Asian context. Wright and Black each reports large-scale studies that examine human capital and leadership challenges in Asia and in the world. Wright's data suggest that MNCs operating in Asia have many similar leadership challenges and investments as MNCs operating in other parts of the world. Black's work finds that Asian employees seek a unique value proposition that has both benefits and costs. Wee and Smith each offers great insights into how Asian leadership and human capital should be managed to create sustainable value. Smith offers ideas on how to future-proof and differentiate the leaders. Wee suggests how Asian leaders can be prepared to lead global companies that are not headquartered in Asia. Other chapters are detailed case studies of how organizations invest in and develop leaders and employees for the future.

Understanding and Management of Paradoxes

Collectively, these chapters confirm the paradoxes that we identified in Chapter 1.

- *Recognize and manage at the same time different organization types that exist within the Asian business community*
  Wee, Wright, Yeung and others point out that State-Owned Enterprises (SOEs), Privately Owned Enterprises (POEs) and Multinational Corporations (MNCs) have different histories, strategies and challenges. It is important to be aware of what type of Asian organization is being studied so that leadership can adapt to those conditions. As each of these organization types evolves, leadership must match those emerging expectations.

- *Learn to respect and work within family-centric enterprises while creating professionally managed organizations*
  Wee, Saw, Smith, Pande and others highlight the importance of Asian leaders shifting from family and personally centric skills to professionally grounded leaders. This means leaders need to master the business disciplines of finance, accounting, marketing, strategy and human resources. These leaders need to access the body of knowledge of leadership research and practice while maintaining a sense of family within the workplace.

- *Relish recent successes and renew to prepare for the future*
  All authors recognize the enormous recent growth of the Asian region. They also point out that the future may not be like the past. The future will require renewal and innovation in how Asian companies operate not

only within their markets, but also within the global context. Allowing pride in recent successes to turn into arrogance may hinder future growth.

- *Recognize bureaucratic, hierarchical and political complexity and create flexible, agile and simple organizations*
  One of the fascinating insights of this volume is how growing and large companies like Unilever, Tata Consultancy Services, UBS, Microsoft and CapitaLand have focused on speed and simplicity. A traditional and logical liability of size is slowness, but as these CEOs point out, when large companies move fast, they can dominate a market. Wright's research shows that MNCs with Asian operations can often lead the way in defining and shaping leadership practices worldwide.

- *Gain the internal efficiencies of operating in a protected market and the external responsiveness of a market-based organization*
  Customers increasingly have the power to shape expectations of how companies must adapt. When companies build products or services to meet future customer needs, companies win. When the ability to adapt can be woven into how leaders are defined and developed, adaptation becomes an ongoing process, not a standalone event. Most of these companies attempt to build a leadership "brand" (Ulrich) where the expectations of customers show up in leadership behaviors.

- *Think long term to envision a future and act today to survive the present*
  Tata Consultancy Services explicitly focuses on long-term thinking with no short cuts. Another good case

of long-term and short-term thinking is how Alexandra Health is working to redefine the role and duty of healthcare providers by working on healthy patients who do not come into the hospital, and at the same time, it is also building a rapid response team with SARS or other immediate disease challenges. Most Asian firms have not been infected with the short-term thinking that has plagued Western firms, but this balance of long and short must continue to be balanced.

- *Maintain grace, courtesy and an Asian style, but be rigorous and demanding, and take risks*
  All people are equal, but equity must also occur within organizations. The thought leaders in this volume encourage differentiation as a key challenge for leaders in the Asian context. The CEOs struggle to differentiate employees while respecting the dignity and worth of each individual. This paradox of equity (differentiation) and equality (dignity to all) will continue to be a challenge to Asian organizations working in a competitive world.

- *Invest in future talent and respond to today's talent needs*
  With the inevitability of change, companies are evolving their cultures, strategies, products, services and management practices. As these actions evolve, leaders need to help employees learn and grow. What helped a leader succeed in the past and present may not be what will help the leader and employees perform well in the future.

The management of these (and other) paradoxes will be a source of ongoing challenge and opportunity for Asian leaders.

Integration and Next Steps

In addition, the chapters offer insights into some of the challenges we identified in the introduction.

First, leadership demand. How important is leadership in Asia?

Without question, everyone in this volume suggests that leadership matters for organizations overall and for Asia in particular (not a surprise since this was the focus of this roundtable). The demand for leaders comes from changing external business conditions around change, demographics and customer expectations (Pande). Without strong leadership, Asian companies may not be able to grow as they have grown in recent decades (Smith, Wee, Yeung). Leaders offer a unique competitive response to meeting customer expectations (Black). It is interesting that while Asia is unique, there are common global demands for MNCs working to build leaders (Wright). In addition, Asian leaders have been more likely to succeed in SOEs and POEs than in MNCs (Wee).

Leadership in Asian organization builds both individual ability and organization capability. Individual ability comes when people throughout the organization have the competence and commitment to do the work expected of them. As companies change either to be more innovative (Alexandra Health), to manage costs (Microsoft), or to find new solutions to consumer expectations (Unilever), the competence of individual employees must change. Leaders help source, develop, reward, communicate with and organize individual employees so that they can be competent and committed. The employee value proposition (Black) or mutual invest-

ment (Yeung) suggests that leaders help employees get their personal needs met when they deliver on company goals. Developing individual talent is a core philosophy and value of all of these companies. The development of individual talent shows up in both succession of senior leaders and development of all employees. Succession implies that leaders as individuals are less important than leadership capability within the organization (Ulrich). Leaders who build leadership for the next generation ensure that leadership is sustainable. But, throughout even large organizations, it is critical that all employees share not only the vision but an understanding of how their personal actions help deliver this vision. Employee engagement (UBS), communication (CapitaLand), development (SMRT) and differentiation (Smith) come when leaders focus on individuals. One of the emerging individual trends is to pay attention to diversity, helping employees come to respect and draw on insights from employees who are different from them (UBS, Microsoft). Another trend is for leaders to focus on what is right, not what is wrong (called a positive approach to leadership) (UBS).

Leadership in Asian organizations also builds organization capability. An organization capability is what the organization needs to be good at doing what it is known for and what customers and investors pay for (Ulrich). Organization capabilities become the basis for a firm's brand. At Tata Consultancy Services, they want to be known for knowledge (expertise) and speed. CapitaLand seeks to be a lasting company. Alexandra Health is shifting towards innova-tion in healthcare services and delivery. These organization capabilities become outcomes of high-quality leaders. Leaders develop a portfolio of HR practices that weave around these capabilities to ensure that the capabilities are institutionalized and sustained. These capabilities also shape the leadership behaviors that help a company succeed.

Leaders matter and leadership matters more. Leaders build individual ability and organization capability that help build successful organizations. When these individual abilities and organization capabilities are woven into the next generation of leadership, organizations will have sustainable success.

A takeaway from this volume is to build a leader scorecard where individual leaders are accountable for how well they deliver results and how well they deliver results in the right ways. In addition, a leadership scorecard would look at how well individual leaders build individual talent (measured by productivity, retention, commitment) and organization capabilities (speed, culture, innovation). These metrics will help create a sense of urgency around leadership as a critical source of competitive advantage.

Second, leadership-shared responsibility. Who is responsible for leadership and human capital development?

At some level, every individual is responsible for his or her own personal and leadership development. The companies in this volume have each explicitly designed and invested in leadership. Tata Consultancy Services sees future talent and leadership as a key to their future success (Pande). SMRT has seen leadership development as a key to their becoming more innovative in their market (Saw). At Microsoft, investment in human capital will help them move from serving one billion to five billion people (Tan). As Alexandra Health grows, the quantity and quality of leadership will have to expand to meet changing healthcare needs. Black does a wonderful job capturing the employee value proposition where the company is obligated to offer employees leadership, jobs, rewards and company reputation. In return, employees are expected to commit their discretionary energy to work. His research shows that when this employee value proposition exists, employee retention and performance goes up. Yeung calls this employee value proposition in Chinese firms a "mutual investment."

The takeaway of this volume is that leadership investment and development is a team activity. Line managers, including those on Boards of Directors (Wee), are ultimately accountable for spending time and effort on leadership. In some studies, top companies for leadership have leaders who spend 30 percent of their time on leadership efforts. The fact that CEOs of these companies attended the Roundtable, wrote their chapters, and are intimately involved in their company's leadership work offers very concrete examples of the importance of leaders in building leaders. HR professionals also play a key role in shaping leadership architectures. Chief Learning Officers move beyond best practices to integrated best systems where the HR work combines to groom future leaders. Outside advisers offer unique insights and share lessons from other companies to shape a leadership agenda. Ultimately, employees are responsible for their own development. They give their discretionary energy and best efforts. When each of these different stakeholders collaborates, the quality of leadership increases.

Third, leadership grooming. How do we groom and develop future talent?

There are some wonderful cases in this volume of how to develop future leaders. For example, Yeung and Smith each suggest some general processes for building leaders. Based on this work, developing future leaders follows a four-step model.

1. Theory or definition. Leadership begins with a clear statement of what makes an effective leader. This statement becomes the standard and turns into behaviors that characterize what future leaders must know and do. A number of companies have worked to define the competencies of effective leaders in the future:
   - Unilever: Future leaders will respond to change by benchmarking honestly against the best and helping to make change happen.
   - UBS: Future leaders will exercise positive leadership for themselves and others with a focus on diversity and community affairs.
   - CapitaLand: Future leaders will enact "building for people to build people" by focusing on attracting people, doing performance management, encouraging staff communication and developing leaders.
   - Alexandra Health: Future leaders will have energy, edge and execution, coupled with uncertainty, vision and innovation.
   - Tata Consultancy Services: Future leaders will be agile, think long term and act short term, groom future leaders and use speed as strategy.
   - SMRT: Future leaders will have mind-view, heartware, relationship, resource, values and people.

Ulrich attempts to capture these competencies of future leaders as a leadership code. Asian leaders, like leaders in other countries (Wright), need to be strategists, executors, talent managers and human capital developers. They need to demonstrate personal proficiency.

2. Assessment. Leaders must be assessed so that they know how they are doing. Without assessment, the standards have little impact. Assessments are like mirrors that reflect how leaders perform in different settings. An assessment requires differentiation based on performance and behaviors. Smith suggests that differentiation is a key future challenge for Asian leaders who often come from a conformity culture. Yeung offers the cases of Portman Ritz-Carlton and Alibaba.com who work to maintain values while having a differentiated talent management strategy. Assessing leaders also highlights the important of high potential which is one of the practices Pande recommends from Tata Consultancy Services. The outcome of assessment is differentiation of employees, which is practiced at CapitaLand.

3. Investment. Companies must invest in grooming future leaders. This includes hiring the right people (see Unilever case), running formal training programs (see cases of Alexandra Health, CapitaLand, SMRT and Microsoft), building more cross-company leadership academies (Wee), and rotating job assignments (Microsoft). There are many ways to develop future leaders, and good companies use a portfolio of options because what works for one individual leader may not work for all.

4. Follow up. Improving leadership requires consistency over time. All of the companies in this volume invest in future leaders with integrated, consistent and sus-

tainable management practices. The myMicrosoft example is a good exemplar. Five HR practice areas (performance management, rewards, career development, management excellence and workplace) are integrated and aligned to develop future leaders. When line managers and HR professionals work with these five HR practice areas, they offer an integrated approach to leadership.

By following these steps, Asian companies may begin to develop the bench of future leaders who can respond not only to Asian requirements, but also to global requirements (Wee).

Takeaways from this volume suggest that organizations have explicit employee value propositions (Black and Yeung) where employees know what is expected of them and what they get from doing good work. Companies also should have clear talent management systems (see for example Microsoft's annual talent management process). These annual processes offer systematic and timely activities that show a commitment to building talent. They are not isolated, but integrated events, chaired by line managers who pay personal attention to leadership development. Organizations also need to integrate their HR practices around consistently building future leaders. These practices include hiring to bring good people into the organization, training programs to help people learn new skills, development experiences to learn by doing, performance management to differentiate employees, rewards tied to performance, and communication to share how work is done. When these discrete best practices are woven together into best systems, leadership grooming occurs.

Fourth, sharing practices and systems. How do we learn from one another?

One of the temptations of leaders wanting to build better future leaders is to identify one innovative idea and adopt it into their company. This volume offers dozens of insightful and innovative best practices on human capital and leadership. But adopting a best practice is dangerous and misinformed.

First, best practices should be adapted, not adopted. What works in one company may not work exactly in another. The myMicrosoft system obviously helps Microsoft integrate its HR practices into an online tool accessible to all employees. But blindly copying this software into another company will not work. The adaptation of practices is reflected in Tata Consultancy Services' business model and they have applied it within their own company. Their commitment to agility, long-term development and strong values directs their consultants to adapt principles to offer unique client solutions. Leaders in Asian operations should diagnose their organization's heritage, customer demands, strategy, culture and leadership styles to adapt current leadership thinking to their organizations.

Second, best practices work together to deliver value. Each of the companies in this volume offers integrated solutions to building talent and leadership. SMRT shows how leadership development begins from the time an employee enters an organization through one's career as individual contributors, managers and senior executives. Best practices need to be replaced by best systems where HR practices integrate to deliver individual ability and organization capability.

Third, sharing knowledge should focus on the future, not the past. One leading company we worked for encouraged others to cite visits so that the public market could learn about what this company had done in the previous five to ten years. The executive confided in us that if the market, including competitors, worked to replicate what his company had done in the past, he would always be the avant-garde doing innovative work and others would be playing catch up. Leadership means anticipating, not replicating. Best practices often institutionalize what *is* rather than create what *should be*.

A takeaway from this volume is that leaders need to learn, but learn in the right way. Learning requires being curious, experiential, inquisitive, open to alternatives, comfortable with feedback and constantly working to improve. But learning is more than generating new ideas; it also requires generalizing or implementing those ideas into their organizations. Often, leaders who learn what they should do, fail to do it. Turning what we know into what we do is a challenge many leaders face.

Fifth, leadership change. What is the future of Asian leadership?

All authors in this book call for more attention to the study and practice of leadership. We want to highlight some of what the future might hold to improve Asian leadership and human capital.

- Maintain Asian uniqueness with a global perspective. Wright's work shows that Asian MNCs are part of a global community of companies. Wee's work shows that Asian leaders have legacy and present constraints on their professional development. It is important for thought leaders to combine their work into thought centers. The Ministry of Manpower (MOM) in Singapore hopes to become one of those thought centers for leadership development.

- Bridge academic theory and research and organization practice. Leaders within companies make thousands of choices that characterize how they govern. Leaders with deep knowledge about their industry, customers and company make choices that distinguish and help their organization succeed. Leadership within companies matters. But academics and consultants who work across companies can begin to see patterns of leadership effectiveness. They are not blinded by single experiences, but able to discern and share knowledge across boundaries. At times, those within companies become separated from the experiences of others. At times, academics become more enamoured with theory and data than application. When academic and practitioners come together, both advance. Centers of expertise that bring these groups together can make knowledge productive.

- Build shared leadership institutes. Wee points out that many organizations are investing in building Asian leadership. This includes companies that build training centers, universities that offer programs, and vendors that offer symposia and forums. When these disparate investments come together, leadership growth may jump forward. Removing the boundaries of these separate groups and focusing them on a common agenda may be politically, economically and culturally difficult, but the result may move leadership forward aggressively. In this roundtable, we talked about the potential leadership academy where these groups come together to share investments for future leaders. Such an academy might help future Asian leaders be qualified to succeed in global markets.

- Focus on the future, not the past. Most of these CEOs and thought leaders are focused on what leaders need to know and do going forward. Most agree that the future will require leaders with the ability to craft strategic insights, the discipline to execute them, the capacity to engage others in shaping the future, the willingness to transfer leadership to the next generation, and a personal proficiency that includes integrity, courage, passion, learning agility and emotional intelligence.

Conclusion

Leadership is clearly more art than science. However, by bringing industry, consulting and academic thought leaders together, lessons can be learned that can be adapted to many. We are deeply grateful to those who have shared not only their experiences, but their concerns as well. It is difficult to analyze oneself and share the challenges ahead. The CEOs have been gracious enough to allow access to their companies. The academics and consultants have presented their data and insights from experiences in many companies. Learning means letting go of biases and assumptions and focusing on the future. We hope that the ideas and experiences in this volume will shape leadership discussion and action in Asian (and other) companies.

Index

Index

Index

Index

Index